Picture Me Perfect

PICTURE ME PERFECT

*Self-hypnosis & imaging
for improving your life.*

DENNIS MARTHALER

NEWCASTLE PUBLISHING CO., INC.
NORTH HOLLYWOOD, CALIFORNIA
1985

Editor—Donna Jaffee
Cover/book design—Riley K. Smith

FIRST EDITION

A NEWCASTLE BOOK
First printing April 1985
9 8 7 6 5 4 3 2 1
Printed in the United States of America

To Marilyn Skeesick Griffiths Marthaler,
who nurtures and supports this flame and
gives me the time to work on it. I love you.

CONTENTS

INTRODUCTION

My interest in hypnosis dates back to my years in grade school, when I would spend Saturday afternoons watching horror movies that always seemed to feature seedy-looking characters dangling watches in front of some man or woman who would become rather starry-eyed very quickly. These "villains" would then command the person to commit some illegal act—such as murdering someone whom that person knew and cared about.

I do not know how my interest in hypnosis survived those movies, but it did, though it did enter a dormant period during my high school days. However, when I joined the military, it resurfaced. I also became interested in karate and fascinated in learning about the concept called Ki. As I understand it, a pure power exists within each of us that, when accessed, enables us to perform acts beyond our normal capacities. During my two years in Vietnam, I observed the Buddhist monks—their lives, beliefs, and practice of meditation. These men performed acts of almost superhuman proportion, an ability they attributed to the power they tapped into, a power enhanced by their philosophy and lifestyle.

After my military service, I attended college and graduate school, where I received my degrees in social work. Although my interest in hypnosis remained, no means of learning hypnosis existed in the academic or traditional therapeutic community. Consequently, I had to reach out to nontraditional members of the therapeutic community, as well as to persons involved in associations that conducted hypnosis training workshops across the country.

My training, however, continued to incorporate ideas from Native American and Eastern philosophies; and although most of that which I will introduce to you derives from traditional techniques, it is certainly tinged with the nontraditional. Traditional twentieth-century Western thinking has imprisoned us within the confines of 10 percent of our minds and offers us no way of accessing that other 90 percent. Were we able to do so, we would begin to look at our lives, at ourselves, differently, and we would begin to practice techniques such as those I will present to you.

One day a while ago, I was in a "project" area counseling a lower-class family about some problems they were having. On my way to my car, I came upon some young children playing outside who expressed great interest in my Jeep. En route to another lower-class neighborhood, I saw a number of middle-aged adults sitting on their steps, in a drunken stupor. One of them lay sprawled out on the curb, having reached another level of unconsciousness. Such a sad scene! But it was even sadder to realize that fifty years earlier those drunken men had been bright-eyed children, watching cars go by and dreaming happily of their future. Had they been able to see fifty years ahead, would they have had the strength to go on with their lives? It seemed so unfair, so unjust. And, yet, was it?

Over the years I have come to reject such concepts as "bad luck" and "coincidence." To believe in them is to relinquish our personal power and to refuse to accept responsibility for the consequences of our actions. A corollary of all this is one of the most prevalent diseases afflicting our culture: lack of self-confidence. Lack of self-confidence breeds lack of self-confidence; and because of our pain, we teach pain and instill a lack of confidence in our children.

The program I will be presenting to you will help you tap into your natural confidence. Crises in your life will continue to arise, but not as frequently; and when they do, you will be able to handle them more assertively, more confidently.

So often we mistakenly look for a quick solution to our problems. When we do not find one, we feel cheated, lost, powerless. Although some of you may find a quick solution in the techniques I suggest, most of you will not. What will be required of you is commitment—commitment and hard work. As you repeat the techniques, you will find that your problems will become increasingly manageable. But even more important, new and healthier behaviors will begin to replace the old, unhealthy ones. The aim of these techniques is to teach you to use more of your natural mental power to improve the quality of your life.

Work on my techniques. Commit yourself to them. Talk about the changes they are making in you, for you. Get excited about your life and the options opening up before you.

Picture Me Perfect

When a child is born, he/she is loving, lovable, intelligent, creative, curious, energetic, powerful, gentle, sociable, cooperative. We never lose these qualities, because they are the essence of being human. Our bodies age, but the child within each of us remains the same. Each night the stars are shining, even though on some nights they cannot be seen because of the clouds. So it is with the child within us. What must be done, then, is for the clouds, which we have accumulated along the way, to be cast off. And then the stars within us will shine with all of their brilliance.

CHAPTER I

A NORMAL

LIFETIME OF

EXPERIENCES

During your lifetime, you can expect to build into your life a majority of the following patterns:

- You will eat in unhealthy ways despite how unattractive you begin to look or how unhealthy you become because you will look upon food as your main pleasure and, at times, as your only pleasure.

- You will drink large quantities of alcohol despite the physical, psychological, and social damage doing so will cause.

- You will smoke tobacco, even though it causes bad breath, stained teeth and fingers; casts a dirty film throughout your home and car; creates burn marks on your clothing and furniture; increases the occurrence of minor illnesses and major illnesses leading to death.

- You will continue to purchase alcohol and tobacco for your friends and loved ones despite your knowledge of their dangers.

- You will take numerous prescription and nonprescription drugs during your lifetime despite the accompanying negative side effects.

- You will expect to catch that yearly flu bug (especially if you are with someone else who catches it).

- You will find yourself occasionally depressed, not knowing why.

- You will feel friendless at times, yet unable to go out and make friends.

- You will find yourself in an unfulfilling, limiting job, but will be convinced that you are unqualified for anything else.

- You will be consumed with fears as new situations confront you.

- You will need to lie your way out of others.

- You will find yourself being short-tempered with people, especially those closest to you.

At every one of these times, you are confronted by a belief, a behavior, that can be challenged. It can go unchallenged, or you can consciously determine to do something you have the natural power to do—something positive. Which is your choice?

CHAPTER II

THE UNHEALTHY

CONDITIONING

PROCESS

Below is a drawing that represents three levels of consciousness.

CONSCIOUS-NESS	UNCONSCIOUS	HIGHER CONSCIOUS-NESS

All of us are born with a level of consciousness. It is that part of us that hears, sees, touches, thinks, experiences.

On another level is the unconscious. It is there that past memories, thoughts, and experiences are stored. Also within this area is found everything we have ever been told about ourselves and our potential.

7

On an even deeper level is our real selves, or higher consciousness. It is the part of us that sees clearly and truthfully, that is loving and lovable, wise and knowing, powerful and gentle. It is that part of us that is in touch with the cosmos. Unfortunately, it is that part of us with which we are least in touch. When psychologists speak of peak experiences or self-actualization, they are referring to concepts that apply to getting in touch with one's higher consciousness.

If there existed only the conscious mind and the higher consciousness, we would have few problems in life. However, we must contend with our unconscious, which exerts considerable influence on each of us. The unconscious influences us in two fundamental ways: through repetition and through instruction by an authority figure.

WHEN INFLUENCE BEGINS

Influence begins very early in life. Using hypnosis, I have taken many people back to the moment of their birth. Some people report that their soul remains outside the mother's womb until the birth and then enters the baby's body. Other people, however, assert that their soul is in the fetus for varying lengths of time during the pregnancy. Many of these people can even describe their impressions of that *in utero* experience. What is of most relevance for us is that these individuals have distinct impressions of what had been going on during their mother's pregnancy, particularly the mother's feelings and conflicts, as well as the parents' feelings about the pregnancy. It seems as though many people when *in*

8

utero were able to perceive a broad range of events and feelings both within and around their mother. Although most people have no conscious memory of this, these memories are stored away in their unconscious.

Much that has been written lately about rebirthing theory focuses on the crippling messages we receive during our birth experience. The tugging, the pulling, the change of light and temperature, the fear, the mother's pain—all this is stored within the newborn's unconscious and affects the child as he/she grows.

WHO INFLUENCES US

As newborns, we are small persons in a land of giants. We do not understand the language, nor can we walk, crawl, or even turn over. Because we can in no way take care of ourselves, we are totally dependent upon the older people around us. But we do not receive only our physical sustenance from them. We receive subtle and unsubtle messages about how to feel about ourselves and our potential within the context of our age and sex, and our religious, physical, economic, and social limitations. These messages—such as, "Mary, little girls don't do that," "George, he's black, he's not like us," "Denny, only Catholics can get to heaven"—convey what our authority figures believe we have the right—or lack the right—to dream of ever attaining.

Swami Rama says, "Suggestions of various sorts begin to influence us from the very moment of our birth and continue almost uninterruptedly from all corners for a long time, pulling us in one direction and then in another, and leading us off into different worlds of experience."*

Our age determines who will have the greatest impact on us at that stage of our lives. As children, we are most influenced by our parents, then by other relatives, such as siblings, grandparents, aunts, and uncles. As we get older and leave home, we interact with a great number of different people. First teachers, fellow students, coaches, and camp counselors, and later on employers, friends, lovers, spouses, in-laws, enter our lives. Each one of them continues to feed our conscious and unconscious minds with messages about their expectations and perceptions of us.

However, we are influenced not only by those people with whom we live and work. Just as influential perhaps are the social messages conveyed by all forms of media —newspapers, magazines, and books; television and radio; theater and film. Every sentence we read, every show we watch, has a potent message about how we should look, what we should say, how we should act. We are even told how to treat "unattractive" individuals, the elderly, the poor.

THE CHANNELS FOR MOLDING

We also are constantly bombarded by suggestions about how we should feel about ourselves and our lives. These suggestions are conveyed directly through words and actions, and indirectly through thoughts and feelings.

*Swami Rama, Swami Ajaya, *Emotion to Enlightenment* (Honesdale, PA: Himalayan International Institute of Yoga, Science and Philosophy, 1976).

I remember years ago watching an episode of *The Twilight Zone* in which a man found a penny on the street and, as long as he had that penny, he was able to hear the thoughts of everyone around him. Each one of us holds the penny that gives us those same "magical" powers.

Below is a drawing that represents how different modes of communication influence us.

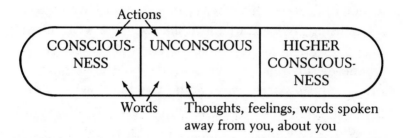

People's spoken words influence us on a conscious and/or unconscious level. Imagine being at a party and chatting with a friend. You are consciously engaged in your own conversation; but unconsciously, you are picking up pieces of conversations that are taking place around you.

Another somewhat related incident almost led to a person's death. David had been hospitalized for relatively minor surgery. He was administered an anesthesia and the surgery was performed successfully. But for no apparent reason, his condition only worsened. The doctors were baffled. David was hypnotized as the last resort in an effort to uncover some reason for his deteriorating condition. Apparently, during surgery, the technicians had been discussing another patient who they said "would not recover." David heard this remark in his unconscious state and thought they were talking about *him*. As a result, he was acting out their suggestion.

Just as we absorb words consciously and unconsciously, so are we affected by others' behaviors. We may be consciously watching one person's actions and at the same time, unconsciously taking in another's behavior. One of my clients, Carl, was an alcoholic and within several months of his death as a result. Because of his weakened physical condition, I agreed to see him at home. Carl and his wife, Debra, did not have a good relationship. While Carl and I talked, Debra went about her chores. No matter what direction she came from, whenever she approached us, Carl would duck for fear of being hit by her. One time he was too slow, and she grabbed a handful of his greying hair and pulled it out. His ducking behavior is an unconscious response to a threat. Consciously, he talks with me, while unconsciously he monitors Debra's location.

Others' feelings and/or thoughts influence us as well, but in a different way. Our unconscious picks up unexpressed feelings and thoughts, and usually stores their messages away. However, from the unconscious, they can influence our feelings about ourselves. Although some people's thoughts are more powerful than others —that is, they exert more influence on us than the thoughts of others—everyone's feelings and thoughts do impact us in some way. Mary had been wanting to lose weight for some time. Finally, she decided to go on a strict diet and increase her exercise at the same time. If she had a group of overweight friends who, as their main activity, went out to dinner together on a regular basis, they would begin to feel threatened by Mary's

12

new regimen. If they went out without her, they might ridicule her attempt to lose weight and even gossip about her because of their feelings of defensiveness and abandonment. The energy generated by this discussion would be picked up by Mary's unconscious and would whittle away at her determination to diet and exercise.

Another example of this type of unconscious communication is reflected in an exercise I have used in my own workshops. One person sits on a chair, closes his/her eyes, and is surrounded by individuals who, on cue, all project a particular emotion—anger, indifference, love—onto that individual. When anger is projected by the group, the individual in the middle often describes the perceived sensations as "pressure," "pains in my body," or a "pushing down on my head." When indifference is projected, the individual describes "coldness" or "sadness," and sometimes he/she bursts into tears. When love is projected, the individual describes the sensation as "warmth" or "being held."

The feelings the group expressed are ones to which we are all sensitive. Once these impressions reach our unconscious, they begin to filter through into our consciousness. A common example of this is when we walk into a room filled with people, and we sense that something is wrong. Consciously or unconsciously, we are picking up the energy of those present. Because energy is attached to thought, one person having negative thoughts can negatively charge the air about him/her. Multiply that by the number of persons thinking negatively, and the result is a room overflowing with negativity. When we enter that room, there is no way to avoid feeling ill at ease.

Although some individuals are more skilled than others at focusing their energy upon those thoughts, we all have the ability to do so. It is therefore very important to examine how we think and talk about others. Do we think and talk in negative and restricting ways that psychically lock others into certain behaviors?

MOMMY, WHO AM I?

As children, we are influenced and molded by those around us, and vice versa. Each of us has a list of rules by which we believe others in our lives should be living theirs, and each of them has such a list for us. We may be aware of most of the rules we set for others; then, again, we may not be. How we can identify these unconscious rules is by listening closely to what we say to others or by observing our feelings about their actions. The same holds true for others' rules about us. Their responses to our behaviors indicate what their rules are.

Every rule we have for every person in our lives changes with age. One behavior that is perfectly acceptable today becomes less acceptable with each year that passes. Parents feel one way about a wet diaper on the five-day-old newborn and another way about wet pants on a thirteen-year-old. As we grow older, the rules change; and all too often, without much reason, the rules are different for different families, classes, sexes, and so on. The normal process of growing up, then, is nothing other than learning how to relate to the environment within the rules by which our older family members have been living.

Listen some time to the rules by which a child is molded: "Don't ask so many questions," "Sit down and be good," "Who do you think you are?" Once when I was in a fast-food restaurant, in the booth ahead of me sat a young woman, who was talking to someone across the table from her. Her two-year-old son had finished eating and was standing next to her on the bench, waving and chuckling at the child behind me, who was having an equally good time. Suddenly, the mother grabbed the boy, sat him down, and told him to "be good." I would have liked to ask his mother why she had disciplined him and what did she think she was teaching him about interacting with others. After all, he was only having a good time with someone his own age, just like his mother was.

As children, we adopt not only our parents' rules, but their attitudes and feelings as well. So often this happens without the parents consciously intending it to. Meryl is a spry seven-year-old who began taking gymnastics classes. While she worked on the bars or did flips in the air, her mother would look on in terror. Many times, Meryl would be present as her mother would tell her friends that she did not know how Meryl could do such stunts because she herself would be terrified. Several weeks later, Meryl quit gymnastics. Had Meryl taken on her mother's fears, or had she suddenly become disinterested in the sport? More than likely, Meryl had absorbed her mother's fears and had slowly begun to incorporate them as her own.

Both of these examples clearly indicate how adults let children know about the rules and feelings that govern

15

their own lives. The injustice is that these children are being molded in directions that are neither healthy nor fulfilling. The immediate results are that the young boy stops his healthy play with the child behind him, and the young girl becomes fearful and stops her gymnastics activities. But the results are long-term as well. The messages communicated to these children enter their unconscious; in the future, anytime Meryl may wish to become involved in some sport, she may feel she first needs to check with her mother, or she may just feel a surge of anxiety and not attempt it. The young boy may begin to shy away from people, thinking being friendly and spontaneous is unacceptable behavior. In essence, then, these children are becoming like the adults who are raising them.

Another story comes to mind about how we learn behaviors and attitudes watching the actions of those around us. Recently reported on national news was the story of a rapist who, at an early age, had learned about sex through pornographic movies. He formed the impression that for a woman to enjoy sex, she needs to suffer. As a result, he raped a number of women, many times torturing them beyond the torture inherent in rape.

Probably over 70 percent of our communication is nonverbal. We observe and interpret the behaviors and attitudes of others; we internalize them; and then we start living them out.

In our society, we have developed the concept of the age of reason, that is, the age by which we know what is expected of us—within the context of our sex, age, religion, and so on—so that our parents feel comfortable about letting us out in public. Presumably, that age is seven. The depressing thing is that most of our rules have nothing to do with our natural selves and, in fact, often distance us from them.

This point will be made clearer as time goes on. As children, we are not aware that these rules are being given to us or that they are being made a part of us. How much do you remember about yourself before the age of seven? It was before that age that you were given many of your rules. People around us, so well meaning, try to teach us what they know about life.

Early in life, our unconscious is filled with the rules and attitudes that mold us into what is supposed to be a good son or daughter, good friend, good student, good person. Throughout our lives we try hard to be happy but so often end up feeling unhappy in our relationships, frustrated and unfulfilled in our work, disconnected from good health, and disappointed in ourselves: the result of carrying within us rules that run contrary to our physical, emotional, and psychological well-being.

We are the stars that shine every night. Unfortunately, the clouds—those powerful, unhealthy rules— have obscured that brilliance. But we are capable of pushing those clouds away.

CHAPTER III

THE FINISHED

PRODUCT:

ADULTHOOD?

All the messages about life we received from others through their feelings, thoughts, words, and actions have entered our unconscious. From there they have molded us without our ever having realized it. A rather humorous example of this concerns some friends of mine with whom I was spending the evening. We had just eaten dinner, and some of us were preparing to get into the hot tub. My thirty-year-old friend Kathy looked shocked and said, "You can't get into the hot tub for an hour." We all asked why, and she replied that her mother had warned her to wait at least an hour after eating before getting into water or else she would get cramps. Kathy said that she had never questioned or tested her mother's words. In fact, all of her life she had postponed even her bath until an hour after she had eaten.

WHAT IS YOURS IS MINE

There was a progression in the way these rules influenced us. First, important people in our lives taught us the rules by which they lived. After years of hearing these rules and having our unconscious filled with them, we unconsciously began to claim them as our own. Most of the time, we forget where or how we learned them.

That is the principle of hypnosis: the repetition of messages until they are absorbed into the unconscious. In terms of learning rules, we actually were hypnotized and were never aware of it. Client after client has told me that they grew up not wanting to be like the adults in their lives, but upon reaching adulthood, found themselves behaving just like those adults did.

I once worked with a family consisting of a mother, Eileen, and her three teenaged daughters: Meg, Shawn, and Jan. Eileen recalls that when she was a child, her brother always forced her to taste his food before he would eat it. He was certain that his food had been poisoned, and he wanted her to test it first. As years went by, she began to develop eccentricities of her own. She became frightened to leave the house. She could not tolerate being in a shopping center, on a bus, or in any crowded area. She and her daughters each had her own bedroom; two were on the main floor, and two were on the second floor. Each evening, they all started out in their own beds, yet by morning they were all sleeping on the living room floor. They were afraid that someone might break into the house in the middle of the night and attack one of them. They felt that safety was in numbers. Meg was afraid to sit in front of the window because she was afraid someone would shoot her from outside. Shawn was afraid to pick up a knife because she feared she would go crazy and stab everyone in the house. They were all afraid to go into the basement because they were sure that someone had broken a basement window, crawled in, and was waiting down there for them. This is a dramatic example of how extreme fear of other people is passed from an older brother to his younger sister, then from that younger sister to her own children. Within this family, the mother experienced the most fear; the youngest daughter the least. But as the girls grew older, the more phobic they would become—the result of all those years of being exposed to their mother's fears.

Another example is Patti, a slender, attractive woman who came to see me because she wanted to lose weight. This made no sense to me, since she stood around 5 feet 6 inches and weighed at the most 110 pounds. We sat down to talk, and I learned that when she was a child, her mother had repeatedly told her that her main asset was her physical beauty, and in order for her to be happy in life, she needed to build her talents around that. Her mother's statements eventually dulled Patti's belief in her other fine qualities, such as her intelligence and winning personality. Patti grew up fearful of losing her physical attractiveness and thus all chances for happiness. Several years after graduating from high school, she entered college but left soon thereafter. Instead, she looked for work in which physical attractiveness was the main requirement. She finally found a job at a dinner club for which she was required to wear a very skimpy outfit as she swung on a trapeze.

Patti has two sisters, who have been influenced in this same way. One sister had been told that her main asset was her intelligence, so she experienced considerable pressure to attend college, graduate at the top of her class, and capitalize on her learning. The other sister had been told that her greatest asset was her personality. None of these women were encouraged in—and in fact, were discouraged from—going in any direction other than that which their mother believed depended on their main asset.

These cases illuminate a point that will be stressed a number of times throughout this book. In our early years, parents have the greatest influence on what will be our expectations of ourselves and our future. The degree to which we are influenced by our parents changes as we enter our early to middle teens. It is at this time that we begin to develop our independence and exert the most influence over our lives as our parents allow us to take on more responsibility for ourselves. But despite how independent we feel, we are still being influenced by the messages we receive from our unconscious. It is these messages that determine how we consciously perceive ourselves; and how we consciously perceive ourselves reinforces what is in our unconscious. Each time we consciously agree with our unconscious, its messages become more powerful and take a stronger hold.

THE TRANSITION, BUT WITH BAGGAGE

As we grow older, we also bring people into our lives who basically share the rules we carry in our unconscious. Shy persons will not develop relationships with people who demand that they be assertive. Smokers do not often spend much time with friends who ask that they not smoke in the same room. By consciously and unconsciously choosing as friends people whose values are similar to our own, we feel we are being supported in the way we are living and so do not feel we have to change.

Marilyn came to me to help her stop smoking. She said that whenever she began a relationship with a person who was a nonsmoker and who would ask her not to smoke in his car or apartment, she would evaluate the relationship in order to decide whether he was worth the effort it would take for her not to smoke.

IS THIS ALL THERE IS?

And so we live our lives, year after year, until something happens that shakes the ill-grounded foundation upon which we have built our lives. Suddenly, we realize that we are not having a very good time, and we believe we should be. Our lives are just not working. And this happens at different ages for different people.

Mark came into my office saying that he was married, had several healthy children, a nice home, a good job, a boat and a snowmobile, yet was unhappy about his life. For many years he had worked hard in order to have everything he had been told he needed in order to be happy; and although he may have felt pleased initially, the feeling had not lasted very long. He found himself becoming bored and listless, and he did not know what to do about it. His confusion and depression could be seen on his face. At times, he said, he even felt guilty for feeling this way. So he began to eat more and thus gained weight. Someone else in his position may have started smoking more, drinking more, taking drugs, having an affair. Another person may have become chronically ill.

LOOKING FOR NEW WAYS VS. HOLDING ON TO OLD ONES

For each of us, the catalyst is different. Amy feels as though she always expends energy on her friends but no one is ever there to help her recharge when she feels depleted. Bob suddenly realizes that his best friend and sole comfort is food or cigarettes. Indulging in either does not make him any happier, and his body only becomes less healthy. Ted feels that his life is falling apart because of a divorce. At some point in our lives something happens that causes us to stop what we are doing and wonder why this is happening to us when we have been following all the rules, or at least most of them. The amount of discomfort we feel will determine the degree to which we are willing to work on the issue.

Jim, a young friend of mine, came to me terribly upset by the news that his sixteen-year-old ex-girlfriend, Carol, had left school and run away from home. She had joined up with a pimp and was now working in a massage parlor, hustling tricks at a local dinner theater, and making pornographic films. She had recently called Jim about getting together; and when they did, he was surprised to see her, elegantly dressed, drive up in a year-old sports car. Jim came to me wanting to know how he could get her out of the business and persuade her to return home. He had asked her the same question, and she had warned him not to discuss it or he would never see her again. I advised Jim to accede to her wishes. For Carol, at this point in her life, the positive outweighs the negative. Were she to have a number of unpleasant experiences—such as being beaten by her pimp or a customer, or contracting VD once too often—perhaps she would realize what her lifestyle was costing her, but not until then.

Unlike Carol, Jill sought help, although somewhat reluctantly. Jill had been suffering from plantar warts for years. She developed them on her fingers near the nails, and they were both uncomfortable and unattractive. Although she had received medical treatment, the warts always returned within three months. Plantar warts have some psychic similarities to boils, which I mentioned to her. She admitted that she had frequently gotten boils in the past, but as the boils had disappeared, the warts had emerged. I began asking her about her past. She asserted that there was nothing bad about her childhood, although "it had been strange." When I asked her what that meant, she very reluctantly began telling me that her father used to abuse her, "but nothing bad." I asked her how bad, and she replied, "He used to punch me until I bled or until my butt was black, but it was nothing like what other kids got." Earlier in the conversation she had told me that she was a "real quiet type of person." From what she told me of her physical condition and past experiences, along with her descriptive statements about herself, it was clear that she had been trained not to complain, not even of her father's physical abuse of her. Her comment that she is "a quiet person" actually means she does not stand up for herself, as she is fearful of other people. As a result, she keeps her feelings about the abuse she received from her father—and from many other men in her life—inside her; and this negative energy works its way out in the form of boils and plantar warts. If Jill does not begin to work out her emotional problems, the negative energy will remain inside her body and will continue to engender illnesses.

The rules by which we live, the ways in which we perceive ourselves, affect us not only psychologically but physically as well. At some point when we can no longer tolerate the pain, we declare that we have had enough and want to change. Whatever the precipitating factor, it comes from unhealthy messages we have received about ourselves.

CHAPTER IV

THREE TECHNIQUES
FOR HEALTH AND
HAPPINESS

Through my practice, I have become increasingly aware that unless we reach the unconscious to correct some of the unhealthy patterns recorded there, change will be very slow and usually not long-lasting. One example is the overweight person who has probably dieted countless times, losing literally hundreds of pounds during his/her lifetime, only to die overweight. The basic reason this person was unsuccessful in his/her attempts to diet is that he/she did nothing to change the information stored in the unconscious.

Because negative, restricting messages present in the unconscious result in unhappiness, lack of fulfillment, and physical ill health, if the process were reversed, if positive, supportive messages replaced the old negative ones, we would experience happiness, fulfillment, and physical health in our lives. In this chapter, I will be introducing you to three important tools for making these changes in your unconscious and in your life; and in the chapters that follow, these tools will be applied to specific problems I feel somehow affect all of us.

THE PROCESS OF HYPNOSIS

In the course of my education, I became aware of the power of hypnosis. Hypnosis as practiced by a therapist is a systematic way of quieting our bodies and our conscious minds so that our unconscious is accessible to new input. The process of hypnosis relies on authority and/or repetition. At this moment, we are the most influential authority figures in our own lives. We believe more in our own self-perceptions than we do in the ways others see us. If we tell ourselves something often enough, we will eventually begin to believe it; and we begin to believe it because the message enters our unconscious, which in turn influences our conscious minds.

I realized in my practice that the client did not have to be in my office with eyes closed, deep in a trance, for change to be effected. Instead, if the person could learn several basic hypnosis techniques, he/she could apply them in his/her own life. The techniques include the following:

- Imagining yourself being the way you wish to be
- Using affirmations while you are in a peaceful, quiet state
- Talking about yourself in positive ways, especially at emotionally charged times

POWERFUL POSITIVE IMAGERY

The following is an example of how the first technique operates. A study was done in which three groups of high school students were selected at random. Each group was tested on free throw shooting, and the results were recorded. Group A did not touch another basketball for two weeks; they were then retested, and their shooting percentage remained the same. Group B practiced an hour a day for two weeks; when they were tested again, they had improved by 24 percent. Group C did not touch a basketball for two weeks but instead spent an hour each day in a quiet place with eyes shut, imagining themselves shooting perfect free throws. At the end of the two weeks when they were retested, their percentage had increased by 23 percent.

Group C's visualizations of successful free throw shooting entered their unconscious, which could not distinguish between actual free throw shooting and visualizations. When Group C was retested, their unconscious had only the memory of having successfully shot free throws and consequently directed the body to repeat this behavior. The principle behind this study indicates that our unconscious does not analyze the messages it receives but instead processes them through to the conscious mind.

We can reap the same benefits by using this technique to change any type of behavior. By visualizing ourselves doing an activity perfectly, our performance will start to improve. This technique can be applied in dealing with all the issues that will be raised in the following chapters.

I recommend the following procedure: Find a time or a place that is quiet. Your time should not be rushed or interrupted. You may want to take the phone off the hook and instruct those you live with to leave you alone for a while.

Sit or lie down in a comfortable place. If you find yourself falling asleep, change the time you have set aside, your position, or location. If you have set aside some time close to bedtime, you may want to reschedule this visualization for earlier in the day. If you have chosen the bedroom, you may want to consider the living room or study. Many times the connection between closing your eyes and being in your bedroom late at night leads to sleep. Play around with it until you find a time and place that feel right for you.

If you are going to use this technique at any time other than in the morning before you get out of bed, you may wish to do a relaxation exercise before you begin. Compose a short sentence, something like "My body and mind are relaxed," and repeat it for a few minutes. Or imagine yourself somewhere totally relaxing for you—curled up in bed on a cold, rainy day, dozing on and off, or stretched out on the beach under a warm sun, listening to the rhythm of the waves coming up on the sand. Imagine yourself at that place for several minutes. As you do, your body will start to quiet down. You will feel relaxed because your memory of that restful scene will remind your unconscious how relaxed your body felt. In turn, your unconscious will cause your body to feel as if it were actually there again.

Another way of relaxing yourself is to repeat the following statements: "I am not my thoughts. I am not my feelings. I am not my body." After repeating these sentences for three minutes, you will begin to notice a quietness filling your consciousness.

Once you have completed this relaxation process, your awareness will have shifted in such a way that you can invest more psychic energy in your visualization. There will be times when you can skip the relaxation process and go directly to visualizing yourself as you wish to be, but you will have more energy for the visualization if you have completed the relaxation process first.

Next, visualize yourself as you wish to be. Do not settle for mediocrity. I want you to picture yourself perfect. If you are giving a speech, imagine yourself onstage, talking beautifully, exciting the audience, catching their interest. If weight is your issue, imagine yourself with a beautiful, healthy body, and imagine confidently refusing those foods that caused you to become overweight in the first place. As these positive visualizations enter your unconscious, they will begin to melt away some of your old negative self-impressions and will help you develop positive, healthy behaviors.

Some of you may have some initial difficulty visualizing yourselves. Do not be too concerned. Some people simply are more visual than others. If you have this difficulty, here is a technique that will help you. Picture just one component of the scene. If you are a baseball player trying to feel more relaxed at bat, start out seeing only the bat in your hands. Focus on its length, color, shape. For now, combine seeing with feeling. Feel your feet in the batter's box in a relaxed stance. Feel the correct positioning of your body. Tell yourself that the pitcher is throwing the ball. See the bat go around. Feel the movement of your body. Know your movement is perfect for this pitch. Feel the bat making contact with the ball, the ball being sent to an open area of the field for a hit. As you begin to feel comfortable with seeing one component, start seeing a second, then a third. Eventually, when you feel comfortable with this, you will be able to visualize the entire picture. Even though at first you may not be seeing everything, you are nonetheless reaping the benefits of this technique.

THE POWER OF THE SPOKEN WORD

The second of the three techniques is one of affirmation. Affirmations are totally positive statements about ourselves and our lives that contradict the negativity we feel. The problems we are currently experiencing have their roots in the unhealthy messages that have been absorbed by our unconscious. Affirmations reverse the process. Once our minds have been quieted, repeating an affirmation will fill our unconscious with positive energy, making it easier to effect positive, healthy changes in our lives.

To perform the affirmation technique, close your eyes, spend several minutes going through your relaxation exercise, and then slowly, in silence, repeat your affirmation. Spend as much time as you need repeating it. You may vary the procedure by closing your eyes, performing the relaxation exercise, and then picturing yourself in the setting that pertains to your affirmation. As you make this visualization, repeat the affirmation to yourself in silence.

RELEASING THE SHACKLES OF EMOTIONS

The third technique involves making affirmations about yourself when you are feeling frightened, nervous, sad, or angry. Although this technique differs slightly from the other two, it functions in the same way as do other hypnosis techniques.

When you feel these emotions, you are no longer feeling centered and so unconsciously tune in to every negative piece of self-information that has made its way into your unconscious. When you experience one of these negative emotions, give yourself fifteen seconds to correct the feeling. If you allow the emotion to remain any longer, you allow its memory to enter your unconscious, where it will reinforce your negative beliefs about yourself. However, if within fifteen seconds you respond to it in a healthier way, you will begin to change your unconscious negative beliefs about yourself.

The next time you feel these emotions, compose a statement that is totally positive and supportive about yourself. It should state that you are going to get through this just fine and that you have everything you need to move on in order to have a happy life.

With this technique, you do not find a comfortable spot and close your eyes in order to make your unconscious accessible. Instead, you are relying on repetition and the emotions you are experiencing. These feelings are fully explained in your unconscious and therefore provide a pathway there. Your new statements will follow that pathway and change the old beliefs into positive and healthy ones.

These three techniques can be applied to a broad range of problems: lack of self-confidence; loss of creativity; weight problems; smoking, nail biting, and other bad habits; poor sports performance; and illness and death. Each of the following chapters will focus on one of these problems and will use the three techniques to correct it.

Before we begin, it is important to realize that having these problems places us in an unnatural state. We are naturally intelligent, attractive, loving and lovable, creative, curious, energetic, sociable, cooperative, and healthy. If we have become disconnected from feeling that these qualities describe ourselves, it is because unconscious messages have convinced us so. By using the techniques I suggest, we can eliminate these obstacles to the happiness, fulfillment, and health each of us deserves.

CHAPTER V

RELAXED

AND CONFIDENT

AGAIN

Lack of confidence is one of the most pervasive psychological problems afflicting us today. Self-confidence does not mean acting tough or aggressive. It does not mean being the life of the party or controlling the topic of conversation; nor does it mean sitting quietly in a group, puffing on a pipe. Although many people appear self-confident, beneath the surface they are tense and unsure of themselves. Next time you are on a crowded street, watch the people as they walk along. Often their eyes are cast downward in their attempt to avert the gazes of others. That is fear or lack of self-confidence.

IS LIFE BUT A STAGE?

I recall an actor who came to me to work on his confidence problem. He confided that the only time he felt confident was when he was onstage. I have found this

to be true of a number of actors I know or have counseled. Many of them do not feel comfortable with or
confident about themselves. A role on television or stage
gives them a chance to be someone else, and with that
opportunity they give themselves permission to do or
to be many things they ordinarily would be afraid of
doing or being. They have nothing to risk because it is
not their life, it is someone else's.

In a sense, every one of us is an actor pretending to
be self-confident when most of the time we do not feel
that way at all. Early in life, we become aware of what
situations make us uncomfortable or unsure of ourselves. These feelings derive from the unhealthy messages we have received about our abilities and potential.
Typically, we do not receive the support we need to
work through these feelings, and so we try to avoid those
situations as much as possible. Consider for a moment
the person who has developed a severe case of agoraphobia. His fear becomes so intense that he cannot
tolerate any open space. As a result, he slowly begins to
eliminate from his life those people, places, and situations that cause him such anguish. Finally, there are
very few places where he feels comfortable. Some agora-
phobics are so terrified that they cannot even leave their
homes. Recently I heard actress Olivia Hussey discussing
her bouts with agoraphobia. She said that the doctor she
went to for treatment was married to a woman who had
not stepped out of their house for thirty-two years!

Although that is an extreme case, all of us suffer from
this condition to some extent. Some of us are afraid to
walk into a room alone and may ask the person we are

with to go in first. Others of us are terrified when we think about addressing a group of people. Others feel nervous when they arrive late and have to walk to the front pew of the church. For each of us, there are people, places, or situations that trigger some unconscious fear, which in turn creates conscious tension.

INTROVERSION AND EXTROVERSION

Many of us feel confident, yet our actions belie this self-perception. Carl Jung, a brilliant psychoanalyst, developed theories about and descriptions of the introvert and extrovert personalities. Both are attempts to deal with life in what appears to be a confident way, yet both stem from the same problem: a lack of self-confidence. Extroverts need to control their environment in order to feel safe. To accomplish this, they control the conversation by being the most talkative people in the group, or they attempt to direct the group's activities. Extroverts talk and behave as if their needs and wishes are more important than anyone else's.

As part of a television appearance in Minneapolis, I was to meet with a woman chosen by the show's director from a number of volunteers to work with her on her weight problem on the air. After a month, we were to come back on the show and discuss the results. The evening before the first show while I was talking with the host, the woman who had volunteered walked onto the set and immediately took over as if the set were hers. She approached the host, who inquired who she was. Without answering, she asked, "Who are you?" During the evening, she provided very little information about herself. Instead, she deflected our questions with humor or threw our questions back at us with a question. These are characteristic examples of the extrovert personality taking charge and changing the subject so her felt inadequacies cannot be seen.

Introverts also lack self-confidence, but they deal with the problem in a completely different way. Because they have been told not to trust their own ideas, they are afraid to talk for fear of people mocking them or belittling them. Introverts often will sit quietly apart from the group in an attempt to very carefully understand the rules of that particular situation. They believe that once they understand the rules, they can feel safer about interacting with those present. The problem is that they never feel they know the rules well enough. As a result, they continue to be very quiet, expressing little and missing out on much that life has to offer.

Phil, who is an introvert, came to me because his wife was threatening to leave him unless he changed. As he described his circumstances, his physical appearance told me much more. He would talk to me for as long as five consecutive minutes without once looking at me; then, very quickly, he would sneak a peak, then just as quickly look to the floor. As he sat in the chair, he looked as though he were trying to make his body as small as it could be: His legs were tightly crossed, his arms were folded into his chest, and his shoulders and head were directed down. In addition, his answers were slow and his words painfully chosen. He looked dirty, and his hair was uncombed and greasy. He worked as a bicycle repairman, and he felt that his boss frequently took advantage of him, at times even cheating him out of money. Phil would sit quietly as his dignity was attacked, never daring to seriously think about complaining or venturing out to find another job. Phil embodies the classic example of an introvert—one who experiences great uneasiness talking about himself, who tries to go unnoticed by the way he carries himself, and who fails to stand up for himself.

ROAD BLOCKS TO HEALTHY LIVING

Below is a list of characteristics that pertain to introverts or extroverts. Look through the list and determine how often you find yourself acting in these ways.

- Having difficulty giving and/or receiving compliments
- Having difficulty looking into other people's eyes
- Having difficulty defending yourself
- Having difficulty completing projects
- Having difficulty setting goals for your future
- Preferring that someone else speak on your behalf
- Having difficulty entertaining yourself
- Needing a few drinks before you can approach a particular person or attend a particular activity
- Eating when you feel sad, angry, afraid, or bored
- Needing to always have your way
- Interrupting others in order to express yourself
- Bullying other people

Some of us may try to rationalize or defend these behaviors, but that does not change the fact that they all derive from a lack of confidence. None are healthy; none produce happiness. How do we lose our self-confidence? Let us look at Jane, who is divorced after sixteen years of marriage. Jane feels the need to make significant changes in her life, but she cannot decide what these changes should be. A "quiet person," once she was married she did not work outside the home. Her husband supported her financially, made almost all the decisions, and was the spokesperson for both of them. Now that she is on her own, she does not feel competent to make any decisions, particularly major ones, nor does she have a clear view of what will make her happy.

Below is a drawing that represents Jane's unconscious, or the unconscious of any person who lacks self-confidence.

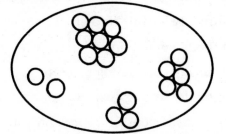

The circles within the drawing represent messages that were absorbed by Jane's unconscious up to this point in her life. Similar messages bind together forming what we call complexes. The larger the complex, the more controlling it becomes. Let us look at some of the messages that form Jane's complex and that led to her present confidence problem. These messages are communicated through the memories Jane has of her past and the important figures in it. One memory is that of her homebound mother, who depended upon Jane's father for financial security. Another is also a memory of her mother, this time as a recluse after Jane's father's death. Then there is the memory of Jane's husband, who because of his own insecurities invariably would ridicule her suggestions and opt for his own. Another memory is that of her brothers, who were always favored over Jane. Finally there is the memory of Jane herself deprecating her own ideas and ignoring her own needs.

The messages conveyed by these memories, together with many other messages she has received throughout her life, have had the following results: Jane has begun to develop what she describes as a "quiet personality"; she feels that her ideas are inferior to those of other people, especially men; she is quiet in group situations as she listens to what others have to say; she demeans her own thoughts and feelings; she increasingly relies on others, no longer taking responsibility for herself; and she acts dull and helpless.

A CONTINUUM TO JOY

Look at the continuum below. In an unhealthy environment, Jane slowly lost sight of her own power as she lost touch with her knowledge of what would bring her happiness and fulfillment. This is what happens to all of us at some time in our lives and to varying degrees. The more we accept the oppressive ideas of others, the closer we move toward the unhealthy end of this continuum. By ignoring our own intelligence and creativity, we increasingly rely on what we mistakenly perceive as the creativity and intelligence of others.

41

HEALTHY

↑

You know what will make you happy, and you go after it.

|

You know what would make you happy but need a lot
of encouragement to act on that knowledge.

|

You know what would make you happy but would not
dare take any action to bring it about.

|

You have no idea what would make you happy.

|

↓

UNHEALTHY

What do we have to do to get back on track? We are
on track; we simply do not realize it. After all, we are
naturally self-confident. The only way we can lose touch
with those feelings of confidence is by accepting negative, non-supportive messages.

We have the tools we need to reconnect with our
feelings of self-confidence. First, we must visualize ourselves the way we want to be.

Visualizations

Find a comfortable, relaxing place where you can sit
or lie down. If you choose, do one of the relaxation
exercises I presented in Chapter 4. With your eyes
closed, picture yourself exactly the way you want to be.
Let's say there are people in your life—your mother,
husband, children, employer—who do not take you seri-

ously, who do not give you the respect you deserve, who do not listen to what you have to say, and you have not been acting assertively to correct this. Visualize yourself with any of them in an appropriate setting (at home, work) acting exactly the way you want to act. If the person is your mother, imagine yourself telling her about the anger and sadness you have felt in the past when she has failed to take you seriously. Picture yourself saying exactly what you wish to say. The only rule is that you cannot imagine yourself being physically abusive.

I remember working with Jennifer, a client of mine, on this visualization. In her visualization, as she began expressing her anger to her mother, her mother ran into the next room. Jennifer had to chase her mother around the house before her mother settled down and listened to what Jennifer had to say. It was a true test of her assertiveness; once Jennifer did this visualization, she began to act more assertively in her mother's real presence and to feel more self-respect. Because of the difference in her interaction with her mother, she was no longer filled with anger when they were together. For the first time in her life, Jennifer was able to develop a healthy relationship with her mother.

Affirmations

The second technique is one of affirmations. Let's consider Jane again. Her affirmations need to address her pattern of quietness and lack of self-confidence. They need to completely contradict the negativity of her self-perceptions. An affirmation for Jane could be one of the following:

"I have beautiful ideas on how to live."

"I have new ideas every day."

"People want me to share my ideas with them."

To perform the technique of affirmations, Jane would find a comfortable position and close her eyes. If she had time, she would do one of the relaxation exercises. She would then slowly state her affirmation over and over again. She would not rush through the words but would repeat them to herself or aloud, slowly and confidently. With time, this new, healthy message would sidestep her objective conscious mind and find its way into her unconscious mind. In situations that were once frightening for her, she would be able to think of healthier and more assertive ways to live her life.

Positive Statements at Emotionally Charged Times

A student has a final exam scheduled for the following week. When he thinks about it, he feels tense because he did not do well on his last one. This moment of tension is an important time. What the tension is saying is "I am not smart enough to do well." Because the student does not feel smart, he worries about his performance. This clouds his mind, and he cannot store information as well as he is capable of doing. As a result, his grade on the exam is not as high as it could have been.

It is very important for this student to come up with a totally positive and supportive statement about his studying and his abilities. The statement needs to completely contradict his worries. Examples would be "My mind is open and clear" or "I am intelligent, calm, and thoughtful." He must repeat his positive statements several times when he feels tense about an upcoming exam, as well as when he walks into the examination room. He needs to make this positive statement within fifteen seconds of feeling the fear. Of course, it is valuable for him to repeat his statement at any time, but the effect is most potent the earlier he is aware of the problem.

Repeating a positive statement during this emotionally charged time will counteract his negative attitude and fears, thereby making him feel positive and reducing the possibility of a self-fulfilling prophecy. It also will quiet his nerves so that when he does study, his mind can store the information efficiently. Finally, the repetition will calm him so that during the exam, he is relaxed and can easily access the information his mind has stored.

SUPPORT EQUALS SUCCESS

What can you expect from people in your life when you begin to act confidently? Unfortunately, you may be disappointed in their response, since some of these persons have a vested interest in your lack of self-confidence. You may think that sounds crazy, but it is true.

Let's look at Jane once again. Her husband did not want her to act confidently. He did not have much confidence in himself, so he certainly did not want her to be self-confident. By strongly encouraging Jane to be quiet, nonassertive, and submissive, he could feel confident. However, what he was feeling was only superficial confidence; it was neither healthy nor long-lasting.

Some people will not be able to handle your new-found self-confidence. By either avoiding you or by becoming angry, they will increase their efforts to force you to return to your nonassertive, unconfident self. For example, your spouse may yell more often, your children may complain that you are not the same person. These behaviors result because you are changing what was the foundation of a comfortable but unhealthy relationship with them. It is important for you to realize that this kind of reaction may happen; and if it does, it is equally important that you repeat your positive statements to yourself. Visualize yourself interacting with these people in healthy ways. Picture yourself with whomever it is in a place where you feel comfortable. Imagine yourself explaining to this person that you are making a change and that you need and want his/her support. Express whatever comes from your heart.

Some people may no longer want you in their lives because they do not like the ways in which you have changed. This is sad, but it does happen. Remember, however, that if their friendship depends upon your being nonassertive, unconfident, and unfulfilled, the friendship is not worth the price you would have to pay for it to continue. At some point these people may come around, but they cannot accept you right now. Do a visualization about them. Again picture yourself with them in a comfortable setting. This time imagine yourself telling them that it is necessary to your growth and happiness for you to make these changes. Tell them that you love them and wish them the best. In your visualization give them a hug and imagine yourself walking away. You may find this experience extremely emotional, but do not let that scare you. If you become emotional, experience the feelings and then move on. It will make it easier for you in reality to change in the ways you wish to change.

Whether you are an extrovert or introvert, here are four simple rules for becoming self-confident. You can apply all of these to the three techniques presented above.

- Believe that you are intelligent, creative, energetic, and enjoyable company.
- Stand tall, feel your feet firmly on the ground, and look into people's eyes. Smile.
- Listen to what people have to say. Encourage them to talk. Give their views respect even if they differ from yours.
- Present your views on different issues. Remember that there can be more than one way of thinking. Respect your views by sharing them.

By following these simple guidelines and practicing the three techniques that have been presented, you will find that you are becoming a much more spontaneous, convivial person. People will begin to take notice and feel more comfortable being with you. Their warmth will, in turn, support your opening up to the true wealth of beauty you have within you.

CHAPTER VI

REALIZING
YOUR CREATIVE
POTENTIAL

Each of us is naturally creative, and our creative abilities are such that they can positively affect every area of our lives. Yet most of us never perceive ourselves as creative, so we never fully explore the depths of our creative pools. Not even the most gifted—noted artists, great sculptors, celebrated writers—ever realize their full potential.

Often when we think of creativity, we envision someone in a studio, wearing a paint-spattered smock and applying paint to a canvas in ways we do not understand. Without a doubt, there is creativity here, but this is only one arena where it can be found. All of us in our everyday experiences are confronted by situations that call for creativity—considering new career possibilities,

resolving conflicts, selecting a vacation spot, even decid-
ing what to wear. When we find ourselves in these situations, we can either follow what has been done before,
or we can use our creativity to design innovative solutions. Anytime we follow precedent, we choose routine
over creativity. But routine requires no thinking; it de-
mands merely an adequate copier. When we are tied
into a routine, we do not consider other possibilities;
and even if they were to present themselves, more than
likely we would ignore them. Creativity, on the other
hand, involves testing new waters, going places we have
never gone before. It also means allowing answers to
come from the depths of our minds and souls, unmo-
lested and unanalyzed.

When we are born, our creative powers are like the
waters of a raging river: wild and pure. Children are
extremely creative and imaginative. Listen to some of
their stories; watch as they play some of their games.
During the years of our growth, our creativity is molded
in many ways, depending upon our environment. For
some, it is reinforced; for others, it is harnessed. For
instance, historically speaking, girls have been encouraged to be more creative than boys in such areas as
fashion and design, food and food preparation, whereas
boys have received more encouragement to pursue their
interest in sports or the sciences. In some families, interest support is not determined by the sex of the child
but by the interests of the parents. Some parents consider an interest in the arts frivolous and nonproductive,
and these feelings are communicated to their children,
who rarely develop an ear for music or an eye for art.

Unfortunately, by the time we reach our teens, our creative waters are no longer uncontrolled and unpolluted; and as adults, that healthy and vital river of creativity has been dammed and tainted by criticism and lack of support. What is more, if we lack self-confidence, we have problems expressing our ideas and feelings. It is far easier and safer for us to follow precedent or to accept other people's suggestions than it is for us to voice our own preferences.

To offset the currents in our lives that go against our self-confidence and creativity, we need to realize that our creativity, our ideas, are beautiful; that our creativity can be applied in all areas of our lives; and that our ideas are worthy of attention.

Let's look briefly at some of these points. Our creativity is beautiful because it opens up new and healthy ways for us to live by giving us ideas that go beyond the rigid boundaries we may have set for ourselves. What is more, our creativity comes from the depths of our minds and souls, as well as from that part of us that is connected to the cosmos.

Our ideas deserve to be heard, as do those of all human beings. Yet it would seem that an openness to others' ideas is becoming a class issue. Adult ideas are considered more important than those of children; men's more than women's, those of the upper class more than those of the middle class, those of professionals more than those of laborers. Typically, when we are in the "less favored" position, we find ourselves intimidated, self-conscious of voicing a contradictory opinion, judgmental and critical of our own ideas. However, the truth is that our creative ideas are just as beautiful, just as valuable, as another person's, whether she is a corporate president or he is disabled and unemployed.

Creativity is like dreaming. If we encourage our unconscious to send forth a dream and allow our conscious mind to remember it, we will dream and remember. Sometimes, just placing a pad of paper and pen by our beds is all the encouragement that is necessary.

The same relationship exists between creativity and encouragement. One way to encourage our creative abilities is to rely on them for solutions to old and new problems, and to translate those solutions into action. Often we fail to act on our creative impulses because of our lack of self-confidence, because of our fears. As a result, we upset the balance we need to achieve between thought and action in order for our creativity to blossom. Another way to encourage our creative abilities is to share our ideas with someone who will act on them for us. We will derive some vicarious pleasure watching our ideas actualized, and sometimes the successful resolution of a problem will ease our fears and increase our self-confidence so that next time we will act on our creative ideas ourselves.

Now let's apply the three techniques I've introduced to enhance our creativity. Remember, regardless of how dull or uncreative we believe we have become, there is always a spark of creativity inside us that can burst into a bonfire, and its fuel is our own encouragement.

Visualizations

When your creative channels are clogged, picturing yourself being creative in specific situations is an effective way to get the waters flowing again. Not only have I used this technique on my own projects, but musicians, writers, artists, and businesspeople I have counseled have successfully applied it to their own creative ventures.

First, find a restful place. Sit or lie down, and close your eyes. Depending upon time and the amount of relaxation conditioning you have developed, you may choose to do a relaxation exercise. Next, select in your mind a location that is connected to the creative project. If the project is a professional one, picture yourself at work; if it concerns planning for a special weekend at home, picture yourself there. Then imagine feeling fantastic because you have just come up with a fantastic idea. You do not have to come up with an idea at that moment, but visualize yourself acting and feeling as if you have. Imagine yourself sharing your idea with whomever is on location with you. Once you have done this, thank your unconscious for producing such a creative idea, and promise to act on it as soon as you can.

Affirmations

Just as negative words obstruct your creative flow, positive words will unleash it. To use the second technique, you need to compose a totally positive statement about your creativity. For instance, if a writer feels her writing is somewhat stagnant, her statement could be "I write exciting, wonderful stories," or "New ideas are flowing from my mind." If a man is dissatisfied with his income and desires either to find different work or to generate additional income, his statement could be "I am coming up with exciting ideas for finding new sources of income," or "New opportunities are presenting themselves in my life."

To apply this technique in your life, first find a comfortable place and close your eyes. If you wish, do a relaxation exercise. Again, I feel a relaxation exercise is important because it will help you focus more energy on your affirmation. Next, slowly repeat your affirmation for several minutes. Take a few minutes, then, to sit in silence. More than likely, ideas will come to mind during those few moments. If not, there is a good chance that within the next twenty-four hours they will. When they do, accept them happily so that your river of creativity will continue to flow.

Positive Statements at Emotionally Charged Times

At times during the creative process a wave of emotions may wash over you. This may happen when the challenge to be creative is first presented to you or later, once you have accepted that challenge. You may experience a sense of fear. Perhaps you have never been challenged in that way before, or perhaps you have been and you failed. Other negative feelings may arise later on. You may come up with some ideas but begin to feel negative about them because you are unsure how to effect them. At the end of the creative process, once it is time to present the completed project, you may lose your self-confidence or become overly concerned about other people's reactions.

If at any time during the creative process you feel negative emotions—sadness, anger, fear—you need to make a positive statement to yourself about yourself, your abilities, and your ideas. Let me illustrate this technique for you. John is given the project of developing a new marketing program for a specific product. This is a project he wants very much because he is trying to prove himself within the company. Early on in the project, John begins to wonder if he has the creative ability to meet the challenge before him. At those moments when he feels doubt, he needs to repeat his affirmation —"I come up with fantastic ideas"—until the good feelings from this statement replace the negative ones. Because negative feelings interfere with the creative flow, he must encourage positive ones, which will allow the creativity to flow again.

SUPPORT: A KEY INGREDIENT

Support is essential to the creative process, and you can give yourself that support by using the three techniques. But the reactions of others to your creative ideas is important as well. Let me give you an example from my own life. I decided I wanted to write this book, but I did not know anything about agents, publishing houses, and so on. I asked myself how I could learn what I needed to know, and the idea of asking the owner of a bookstore came to mind. Armed with dozens of questions, I approached a bookstore owner with whom I was acquainted. Instead of the encouragement I had expected,

I was greeted by depressing information about how most good books never get published and how most writers cannot find a publisher who will even look at their manuscripts. Feeling totally dejected, I left the store.

I then decided that the most productive action I could take was to make positive statements about my idea and leave the negativity behind. A week later, I was teaching a class in which one of the students happened to be involved in publishing. He gave me a great deal of professional advice, as well as magnificent support.

You do not have to accept the negative responses of others to your creative ideas. If you present your ideas to someone who replies, "You can't do that," you have three courses of action: (1) you can walk away from that person, and tell yourself that your idea is fantastic and has a lot of promise; (2) you can tell that person that you want positive information and support. If he/she cannot meet your needs, you cannot be with him/her; or (3) you can change the subject, and realize that because of that person's own fears and lack of self-confidence, he/she cannot give you what you want. Tell yourself that your idea is creative and viable.

Hold on to your creative energy. Trust it. Use it. Life is enhanced because of it. Apply the techniques I have given you, and judge the results for yourself.

CHAPTER VII

BEING

NATURALLY

SLENDER

We are naturally slender. This statement may be difficult to accept when we consider our never-ending battle with our weight. If we look at people in any crowd, we realize that most of them, especially those over thirty, could stand to lose a few pounds. That extra weight places greater stress on their bodies' systems, interferes with their participation in physical activities, and causes them to look and feel less attractive. Although eating is necessary and brings such pleasure, eating incorrectly has a very high price.

A former patient of mine who weighed close to 300 pounds told me that when she was growing up, her mother would prepare enough food at mealtimes to feed any friends or relatives who might drop by. The problem was that most of the time no one ever did; and the family members, who claimed they wanted to watch their weight, felt compelled to finish off the extra helpings. As a result, everyone in the family weighed over 250 pounds.

UNCONSCIOUS MOTIVATORS FOR EATING

Working with individuals who maintain that they wish to lose weight, I have found that there is always a part of them that does not. It is as if they have split personalities. That part of them that wishes to lose weight corresponds to their conscious mind; that part of them that does not corresponds to their unconscious. The slender personality wants to control its weight so that it can have a healthy and attractive body. The overweight personality, on the other hand, wants to continue eating as much food as it can, for whatever reason. That is why so many people diet, lose their extra weight, then gain it right back.

Certain people, places, and emotions will trigger one personality; other people, places, and emotions will trigger the other. Maybe summer is rapidly approaching, and we feel the urgency to get into shape; or maybe a friend or relative has died from a heart attack caused by excessive weight. The slender personality takes control, and we resolve to diet. But as so often happens, when we become frustrated in our progress, discouraged by the degree of discipline required to stay on our diets, the overweight personality takes over and leads us into temptation.

One of the reasons we eat is because we are hungry. Our bodies tell us that more fuel is needed to keep us going. But for most of us, hunger is the least of our reasons for eating. We eat out of boredom, fear, depression, anxiety. We eat because food is our only source of comfort, of pleasure. We eat because we equate weight with power. We eat to compensate for the emptiness of our pasts. We eat to be social. Sometimes, on holidays like Thanksgiving and Christmas, we eat until we can barely breathe, let alone move.

Although we are naturally slender and usually eat like a slender person eats, there are times when we do not. What follows are examples of how that unhealthy part of us takes control and causes us to eat for unhealthy reasons.

Example One: Soon after Elizabeth married Larry, she began to realize that he was possessive and jealous. Every time the insurance man came to collect the insurance premium, Larry would accuse Elizabeth of having an affair with him. Elizabeth could not tolerate the accusations and eventually called the insurance office and informed them not to send the agent again because in the future she would mail in the premiums. Larry also suspected the milkman, so Elizabeth canceled the delivery service and began buying milk at the grocery store. Yet, despite her efforts, Larry continued to suspect her of being unfaithful. He himself spent a lot of time after work in a particular bar; and when he returned home at night, with slurred speech, he would question Elizabeth suspiciously about what she did while he was gone. (It is interesting to note that in their forty years of marriage, Larry has refused to tell Elizabeth the name of the bar.)

Elizabeth, who at the time of her marriage was quite slender, began to eat more and more. Understandably, she was feeling tense and pressured in her relationship with Larry, and food seemed to make her feel better—less tense and less fearful of what Larry would say to her once he got home. The more she ate, the more weight she gained—and a curious thing began to happen: Larry stopped accusing her of having affairs. She may not have consciously made the connection between her weight and Larry's jealousy, but unconsciously she did. Several times when she started to diet, Larry's accusations would begin anew. As a result, she found that life was more peaceful for her when she was overweight.

Example Two: Gail is a thirty-nine-year old successful businesswoman. She weighs approximately 175 pounds and claims that she wants to reach her perfect weight: 140 pounds. Given her height, this weight seemed a bit high to me. As we talked, Gail realized that previously, when she had gone below 140 pounds, she had become terrified about losing control over her body and becoming promiscuous. She believes this fear is justified because once, when she was on a week-long cruise, she had affairs with three different men. Now, the closer she gets to 140 pounds, the more tense she becomes because of her fear. Staying above 140 helps her feel safer about the image she has about herself and about how she consciously wishes to behave.

Example Three: George is in his middle twenties and lives with his wife and son. Although he eats three well-balanced meals a day, he has a serious weight problem: George consumes vast amounts of food between meals.

If friends or relatives drop by, George automatically serves them cake, pie, ice cream, or some other rich dessert. If he is out with someone, he usually recommends that they stop to grab a malt or sundae. By focusing on his weight problem, George realized that he feels nervous and ill at ease in a one-on-one situation. He has learned that one way he can defuse this tension is to be engaged in some activity, like eating.

Example Four: Ann came to me wishing to lose forty pounds. When we examined her eating patterns, it became apparent that she does not eat much during the day. But once home from work, she does not stop eating. She nibbles as she prepares dinner, and then eats dinner as she watches television. During the evening, she snacks on potato chips, popcorn, ice cream, cake, and candy. She falls into this same routine on weekends, only it begins after breakfast and continues throughout the day. She is not involved in a romantic relationship, she has no hobbies, and she seldom socializes. Work and the pleasure she receives from snacking at home are the only activities in her life.

These people believe that they use food supposedly for their benefit. But if they listened to that healthy part of them, they would realize how destructive their excessive eating actually is to their physical appearance, their health, and their relationships. That healthy part of us tells us that we deserve to be healthy, slender, attractive, and energetic. If we aren't, if indeed we are overweight, we may *pretend* we are not. The overweight personality wants us to continue overeating and at the same time ignore the consequences. It will devise all sorts of behaviors that presumably will hide our true weight from our awareness. These behaviors may include:

- Not weighing ourselves
- Not looking in full-length mirrors (I have met people who have even taken their mirrors off the walls.)
- Not tucking our blouse/shirt into our pants or skirt (Wearing it out hides our waistlines.)
- Wearing certain styles of clothing that supposedly hide our body bulk
- Choosing colors that will have the same effect
- Not undressing in front of our spouse
- Sneaking out at night to buy unhealthy, fattening foods (like chips, cookies, candy)
- Not going to the beach (so we don't have to wear swimsuits)
- Choosing friends who are overweight (The bigger they are, the more they will call attention away from us.)

By behaving in these ways, we are reminded less often of our physical appearance. However, try as we may, we cannot totally conceal our bodies from other people. At some point, we have to think about our eating habits and how we can change them.

Overweight people often feel guilty and different from other people. They shouldn't because they aren't. Unfortunately, we have all been conditioned to believe that we are somewhat powerless in our own lives. When we believe that we are limited in our options, we tend to develop bad habits to deal with our frustrations. Our bad habits are, to some degree, our attempts to make sense out of situations that do not make sense to us. They are a means of getting rid of the negativity we are feeling at particular moments. All of us have developed bad habits, and some are more detrimental to our physical well-being than others. Eating when we are not hungry is one of them.

Regardless of what people in our lives say, we deserve to be slender. We deserve to be healthy. We deserve to realize our image of how we want to look and feel— slender, attractive, and in good physical health. We deserve these things, and we are capable of making them happen for ourselves.

DAY-LONG AWARENESS

Stop for a minute and think about where and when you take in those unnecessary calories. Be honest with yourself. Recently, I worked with Ralph, a twenty-seven-year-old man, who was trying to figure out how he could have possibly put on an extra thirty-three pounds. He works the night shift, from 11:00 P.M. to 7:00 A.M. He eats nothing during that time but does drink three cups of black coffee. He gets home at 7:30 and goes straight to bed. He says that he eats only one meal each day, something like soup and a sandwich—around 7:00 P.M. Occasionally, during the day, he stops to grab a hamburger and fries. That's not much food for him to consume—or to account for the additional thirty-three pounds. However, as we talked, Ralph admitted that every morning when he gets home from work he drinks two beers to unwind; and on weekends, he drinks from twelve to twenty-four cans of beer. Now *that's* a lot of calories, and it shows Ralph how he has gained weight.

At mealtime, some people pile mounds of food onto their plates, or they go back for additional helpings when probably they shouldn't. They also take in a lot of calories each time they snack while watching television, each time they open a package of donuts before work in the morning. Think for a moment about your eating and drinking habits, paying close attention to where and when you take in all of your calories. If you wish, list those places you eat everyday, as well as those places you eat occasionally.

Next, become aware of why you are eating or drinking at that particular moment. Are you eating because your body is truly hungry, or are you eating for some other reason? It is eating because of those other reasons that is making you gain weight. Think of the time you spend eating in terms of energy. If you spend less time eating, you will have additional energy with which you can pursue more constructive activities. Study your eating patterns. Each time you find yourself in one of those situations where in the past you have turned to food, ask yourself what you really want to do at that moment. Do not accept "eat" as an answer. You have to come up with an answer that is healthier, one that stretches your boundaries. The following three techniques will help you deal with these situations.

Visualizations

Every overweight person has an unconscious that is filled with memories of overeating, in all sorts of places, for all sorts of reasons. The intention of this technique is to erase some of those unhealthy pictures and replace them with newer, healthier ones.

Think of several places where you have overeaten. Now sit or lie down in a comfortable spot. Take a moment to calm down, then close your eyes. Go through a relaxation exercise until you can sense a pleasant difference in your body. Now I want you to spend from two to ten minutes picturing yourself in several of the places where you have overeaten. This time, however, I want you to picture yourself either not eating at all or else eating smaller amounts of food. If you picture yourself not eating, see yourself engaging in some form of healthy activity. Ask yourself, "What do I really want to do right now?" Eating is out of the question, so wait for another answer to come up. In either case, I want you to feel and act confident about the situation.

Here is an example of what I mean. Pam came to me wanting to lose weight. She is shy, nervous, and easily influenced by others. As we discussed her eating patterns, she told me that one of the most difficult times for her is when her children come home from school. Pam works nights and does not get much sleep during the day. People are frequently telling her that she needs more sleep than she is getting. Although she feels fine with the number of hours she is sleeping, she also feels that instead of sitting at the kitchen table and talking with her children about school, she should be in bed, trying to catch up on her sleep. However, experience has taught her that even if she lies down after 3:00 P.M., she cannot fall asleep. So she sits at the table with her children, eating cookies, drinking milk, and feeling anxious. It is important for Pam to learn what she wants to do, and then to start being assertive about it. Does she want to lie down even if she knows she will not be able to fall asleep? If she does, then she should and be satisfied with just resting. If she decides that she would rather spend the time with her children, then she should do so, enjoy their time together, and ignore other people's advice.

An effective visualization for Pam would be for her to see herself at the table with her children, feeling comfortable, confident, and sharing their day with them. If she chooses, she can picture herself munching on an apple and feeling good about her snack selection. The important point is for her to see herself as changed: relaxed, enjoying her children, and not overeating.

Let's consider Ann again. A visualization for her would be for her to see herself preparing dinner without munching. She should picture herself feeling confident and self-disciplined in this setting. She should also spend some time picturing herself in the evening after dinner, engaged in any activity she thoroughly enjoys—but without food by her side.

Many times we fall into ruts, and we forget that we have the power and the ability to create new and meaningful ways to spend our time. We know that we deserve pleasure in our lives, and food is an accessible pleasure. That is the rut. But focusing on new and fulfilling activities will keep us smiling and feeling good about ourselves.

Affirmations

Also within the unconscious of every overweight person are statements that reflect a feeling of powerlessness regarding loss of weight. Decide on a statement that you feel is powerful and confident, and that signifies a new way for you to look at your relationship to food. Such statements would be:

- "I have changed. I am making my body healthier."
- "I am in control. I eat only for healthy reasons."
- "I am naturally healthy and slender."
- "Every day I am becoming slimmer and trimmer."

Take one of the above statements or compose one of your own. Once you have done this, find a restful place, and sit or lie down. Take a moment to feel comfortable and to settle down, then close your eyes. For several minutes do a relaxation exercise. Once you feel a quietness fill your body and mind, repeat the affirmation you have chosen. Do this silently, slowly, and with feeling. Really experience the statement. Feel as though you already have made the change. Repeat the statement to yourself for two to ten minutes, then stop. The statement, as a result of your repetition, will have naturally entered your unconscious. Open your eyes, and go on with your daily activities. You will find, much to your surprise, that the old habits will not feel the same, will lack their old forcefulness. It also would be helpful for you to repeat your statement to yourself several times throughout the day. In this way, you are reminding yourself of the change you are making.

Positive Statements at Emotionally Charged Times

As we discussed earlier, people, places, or emotions can trigger our overeating. Look at the chart below. Too

often, we believe we have only two options—#2 and #3
—when in reality we have three.

Option No. 1
You deal with the situation effectively and healthily.

Option No. 2
You feel somewhat powerless. You deal with the situation but eat and/or drink alot. This serves as your security blanket as you tackle the issue.

Option No. 3
You do not feel you can deal with the issue, so you do not. However, because of the tension caused by the situation, you eat and/or drink a lot.

By turning to food at emotionally charged times, we strengthen our unconscious belief that we cannot deal with certain situations in healthy ways. However, Option #1 allows us to give ourselves the encouragement we need to handle the situation differently. The next two examples indicate how Option #1 can be used to lose undesired weight.

Janet is single and lives alone. She works during the week, and on weekends she occasionally goes out with female friends. Janet has been in a relationship with Michael for the last several months and lately has been spending the weekends with him. One of Janet's problems with the relationship is that Michael usually determines when they will see each other. As a result, because Janet wants to spend a lot of time with him, she feels frustrated and anxious when he does not call. If the weekend arrives and they have no plans to get together, she worries that he is with someone else and that their relationship is over. These weekends are extremely difficult for her, especially where food is concerned. She finds that the easiest way for her to cope with the situation and to relieve her anxiety is to stay home waiting for Michael to call and snacking to fill the time.

Janet needs to be aware of the times she overeats and/or overdrinks. At these times, she needs to ask herself, "Is this healthy eating?" If she is honest with herself, she will realize that at these times she is experiencing feelings of sadness, anger, boredom, loneliness, or powerlessness. She needs to tell herself confidently that she is in control and then ask herself what she would really like to do. When Janet asked herself this, she found answers like "I want to call my girlfriends and go out," or "I want to call Michael and talk to him about where he sees our relationship going." In both of these cases, she is starting to take control of her life. She is starting to go after what she wants rather than waiting for it to be given to her.

Another example is Jim, who after graduating from college moved to a new town because of a job opportunity. Shortly after he moved, he began gaining weight until he was thirty pounds too heavy. As we talked about where and when he was overeating, it became apparent that after work he would sit down in front of his television and eat the night away. His eating was to compensate for his loneliness and boredom. He had been socially active back in college, but he had done nothing to establish himself in his new environment. He had thought about going out at night or about approaching fellow workers to participate in some activity, but he had always gotten nervous and shied away from taking the initiative. Now he was feeling depressed and wondering whether he ever should have moved.

When Jim feels bored and depressed, he needs to ask himself, "What do I want to do?" and needs to listen to the response. Once he did so, he began to think about the activities he had enjoyed playing while he was in college, such as intramural volleyball. He made some inquiries and was delighted to learn that there were a number of adult volleyball leagues that competed in the evenings at schools around town. He soon joined a team and began playing every Wednesday. Yet when he played, he found that he still felt and acted like "the new man," that he wasn't reaping all the pleasure he could from the experience. Again he asked himself, "How can I make this experience better?" He realized that he wanted to socialize with several of the players after the game. He had been shying away from something like this, afraid that he might be intruding. But when he summoned up the courage to suggest they go out for burgers, the whole team enthusiastically came along.

Every one of us sees the potential of our lives through eyes that have blinders on them. "What else can I do? What do I really want to do?" When you ask yourself these questions, you cannot accept the answer "Nothing." Every situation has its options. Whenever you choose to overeat, you are considering only Options #2 and #3 on the chart; and the only reason you are is because you do not feel powerful enough to choose

Option #1. But you *are* powerful enough to select Option #1, and you will be a lot happier when you do.

SUPPORT MEANS ENCOURAGEMENT

There is another point here that is of key importance and that concerns the support you receive from others. One woman I counseled worked hard and long to lose a considerable amount of weight. As her reward, her husband brought home a gallon of her favorite ice cream. Another woman I know told her boss that she was losing weight, and his response was, "Gee, I like you fat. I don't know if I'll like you thin." What is support and what is not? Many people insist that they are getting support, yet when they look at what they are getting, they realize that it is not support. Those closest to you, those who should be encouraging you and supporting you, are often the ones who are least encouraging, least supportive. Sometimes, this is obvious, but most times it is subtle. Here are some ground rules about support:

- No one has the right to call you names like fatso, buffalo buns, etc.

- You never have to accept a remark like "Oh, you're on another diet? How long will this one last? [chuckle] "

- You have the right to tell your parents, friends, partners, colleagues, that you would rather do something more constructive than go out to a restaurant.

- When you turn down food, that should be it. So often we are bombarded by statements like "Oh, come on, finish this off," or "What is the matter? Don't you like it?" Do not let someone else's ego decide how much you will eat.

- You deserve supportive comments from your friends and relatives on your new self-discipline and improving appearance.

The closer the person is to you, the more closely he/she should follow these rules. You can use the visualization technique to help you handle support. If you are not receiving it, visualize yourself demanding support from that person.

Support is important for all of us. First we need to give ourselves support, then we need to receive it from others. Even if we do not receive it from others, we are still receiving it from ourselves; and in the process, we are telling ourselves that we deserve it from others. When we give ourselves our complete support, we are better able to identify what others are giving us.

I strongly believe in exercise along with a healthy diet. When you go on a diet, your body thinks you are starving it, so it dramatically reduces the number of calories it burns every hour. This explains why some people who only reduce their food intake do not lose weight. There are two ways this can be corrected. The first is to decrease your calorie intake even more. The second is to exercise. When you exercise for longer than twenty minutes, you increase the rate at which your calories are burned off. This rate remains increased not only during the time you are exercising but for a number of hours afterwards as well.

Our society has an obsession with slender bodies. Some of its reasons are positive, others negative. Do not lose weight because of society's pressure. Do it for yourself. As you set your goals, adhere to your regimen; and as you begin to notice a change in how your clothes fit, you will notice other changes as well. For starters, you will have more energy with which to live your new life.

Use my three techniques, and you will find that your true creative faculty will present to you healthier ways with which to use this newly found energy. As you learn to not be controlled by your fears but instead to live through them, thereby eliminating them and the need for excessive food, you will never return to your old unhealthy ways.

CHAPTER VIII

QUITTING

SMOKING AND

LOVING IT

COMMON SENSE GOES UP IN A PUFF OF SMOKE

There is much confusion, much conflicting information, about tobacco. For years, individuals, businesses, and even our government have promoted it. In fact, the U.S. Government pays subsidies to farmers to grow tobacco. The tobacco industry reassures us that there is no connection between their product and illness. Yet we know how smoking affects our breathing, endurance, and the very air we breathe.

Most smokers with whom I have worked on their smoking habit insist that they do not know what causes their morning cough. It is time they learned. Cilia, very small hairlike fibers that have a gentle, wavelike motion, line the passages from our lungs to our throats. Their

75

purpose is to guide any impurities that have found their way into our lungs up into our throats. We then either swallow these impurities or we spit them out. Nicotine paralyzes the cilia and so prevents our lungs' cleansing mechanism from functioning. Therefore, when we smoke, tar and other impurities in the cigarettes are trapped in our lungs. (A person who smokes two packs of an average cigarette a day puts the equivalent of one cup of thick, sticky tar into his/her lungs in one year!) At night, while we sleep, the deadening effects of the nicotine slowly wear off, and the cilia once more begin to remove the impurities from our lungs, in an upward direction. As these impurities are dislodged, our lungs start to feel better.

But then we awake, and we start coughing. Over the years of smoking, many of us have learned how to tackle this ticklish problem. We grab a cigarette, light it, take a deep drag, and like magic our cough is gone. What we have done is to send a new supply of nicotine down to those cilia, paralyzing them once again. No longer can they work at cleaning out our lungs, and that unhealthy accumulation of debris remains. One consequence of this is that smokers, on the average, develop colds, coughs, bronchitis, and emphysema more often than do non-smokers.

What is important here is that our bodies are telling us what is natural and what is not. Our bodies have certain natural cleansing systems. If these systems are prevented from functioning as they are meant to, there can be only unhealthy consequences. So many smokers have said to me, "But I really enjoy it," or "I am as healthy as can be." Although smoking may sensually please us and we may think we are healthy, there is no way we are as healthy as we could be if we did not smoke. We cannot afford to look at this problem on a superficial level. Smoking takes years off our lives, and the quality of the life we do live will be greatly diminished if we continue to smoke.

I want to interject some thoughts here on bad habits. Although having a bad habit places us in an unnatural state, having bad habits is, unfortunately, the norm. As I observed in the previous chapter, bad habits develop as a release from feelings of powerlessness. To ease these feelings, some of us turn to food, others to drink, and still others to smoke. However, it is essential to know that we are not powerless and that there are healthier ways of dealing with tense moments.

THE PHYSICAL ADDICTION

If we smoke, we become addicted, both physically and psychologically. The physical addiction is caused by the nicotine in the cigarettes. When we first stop smoking, we experience cravings for a cigarette between two and four times an hour. These cravings last about three minutes, whether or not we have a cigarette, and will continue for about seventy-two hours (three days); then their frequency will start to diminish.

There are certain things you can do that will help reduce the intensity of these cravings, as well as the time it takes for them to diminish. An increased supply of oxygen can accomplish this. Consequently, whenever you begin to crave a cigarette, increase the amount of oxygen you take in either by breathing deeply or by doing some form of exercise.

Another way to diminish the frequency and duration of cravings is to take very hot baths. This causes you to sweat the nicotine out of your body. Fill the bathtub with water as hot as you can tolerate without burning yourself. Let the hot water from the faucet continue to trickle so that the water in the tub will remain hot. Lie down in the tub with as little of your body out of the water as possible. Then place a towel over your head, allowing the towel to sink into the water. Heat should rise up to your neck and face, causing these areas to perspire as well. You should follow this bathing procedure at least once a day until you feel comfortable with the level of confidence you have achieved about not smoking.

A third way to counteract nicotine buildup in your system is to drink red clover tea or take red clover tablets. Red clover is a simple but powerful red and white flower found in most farmers' fields; you will most easily find it in a health food store. The properties of red clover will cleanse your blood of the nicotine that is slowly poisoning it.

THE PSYCHOLOGICAL ADDICTION

Now to the psychological addiction. When clients ask me to help them stop smoking, one of the things I ask them to do is think about where and when they smoke during the day. In the morning before they do anything else is a common answer, as is while they drink their morning coffee. Somewhere in smokers' minds they recognize all the dangers associated with smoking, yet a number of times each day they throw caution to the wind and smoke. I have found that for most people there are four areas of vulnerability that, when triggered, will cause them to reach for a cigarette. These include certain people, certain places (bars, in the car, on the phone), certain topics, and certain emotions. Look into your life, and start observing what is happening each time *you* reach for a cigarette.

Harold came to me for help with his smoking problem. He was about ten minutes late for one of his appointments, and when he arrived, I could tell he had been smoking because he reeked of cigarette smoke. He told me he was late because he had been attending a meeting in which the guest speaker was taking more time than he had been allotted, having strayed off the topic he was to have addressed. Harold had sat there, knowing he was going to be late and becoming increasingly tense and angry. And so he began smoking. After the meeting, on his way to my office, he felt tense about being late, and he smoked some more. I asked him to consider other alternatives for coping with his anger during the meeting. Below are the possibilities he listed for me:

- Biting his nails
- Tapping his fingers on the table
- Tapping his pen on the table
- Doodling

After he gave me these answers, I asked him if he had thought about doing something healthy, like getting up and leaving the meeting, or informing the speaker that he had exceeded his allotted time and was preventing those present from going where they needed to go. With an amazed look on his face, Harold replied that he had not considered either alternative. That is precisely Harold's problem: He cannot imagine relieving his tension or anger except by smoking.

Smokers feel they have to smoke when they find themselves in highly charged situations, because they believe that they feel better when they do. As this behavior pattern is repeated, the information enters their unconscious, and the habit of smoking is formed; that is, these smokers no longer consciously think about reaching for a cigarette, they just do it. I have asked smokers what they would do in a particular situation if they could not reach for that cigarette. Almost always they have replied, "I don't know."

THE CREATIVE EDGE

To eliminate this psychological addiction, set a date by which you intend to stop smoking. Do not change that date for any reason. Next, think about where and when you smoke. Start with the moment you open your eyes in the morning and go through your entire day. Then, start exploring alternatives to smoking at those times and in those places. Find creative and constructive ways of expending all the energy that you used to invest in smoking.

There is something I call a "now what do I do" cigarette. It is the one you light up right after you have finished your meal. Prior to that cigarette, eating provided a buffer between you and those with whom you were eating. You are together during the meal but not entirely, because much of your attention is focused on eating your food before it gets cold. You are now finished with your meal and are faced with the question, "Now what do I do?" Heavy-duty eaters have ordered a nine-course meal, which consumes any time they could have had to interact; drinkers order a drink; and smokers grab for their pack of cigarettes.

Because you no longer smoke, you need to come up with creative ideas for filling the time you would have spent smoking. One of my clients, Jason, began asking himself after the meal, "What do I really want to do?" There were many things about Hilary, the woman he had been dating, that intrigued him, but he had been too shy to pursue the subjects. Now, he found himself taking a deep breath and asking what he wanted to know. To his surprise, Hilary thoroughly enjoyed his questions. As the conversation began to deepen on subsequent occasions, their relationship deepened, and Jason began to feel totally at ease. Instead of each of them going his/her own way after the meal, Jason realized he would like to extend his evening with Hilary. Whereas in the past he would have been too nervous to spend more time with her, he discovered that, like a child with a new toy, he was looking for new ways to enjoy Hilary's company, his own creativity, and himself. Jason was learning to expand on the behaviors he saw before him. No longer was he willing to be controlled by his fears and his tendency to occupy time with smoking. He was learning that there was a new world and new ways of behaving.

My three techniques will help you be more motivated and spontaneous about making the above changes.

Visualizations

You have already thought about your smoking patterns and are now aware of when and where you smoke. You are naturally a non-smoker. Remember that. Find a comfortable place, sit or lie down, and close your eyes. Do one of the relaxation exercises I have given you or do one of your own. After spending up to ten minutes going through your relaxation process, picture yourself in one of those situations in which you have smoked in the past. This time, however, picture yourself not smoking. Besides not smoking, picture yourself totally involved in that situation. Picture yourself feeling self-confident. If you picture yourself in a social situation, envision yourself confidently asking questions, talking about yourself, and feeling close to the people around you. If you are picturing yourself in a tense situation, see yourself handling the situation confidently and competently, doing what needs to be done, and feeling good about yourself. Visualize yourself in two or three scenes, then sit for several seconds in silence. Tell yourself that you have done just fine and open your eyes.

Seeing yourself as a non-smoker will help you not smoke. Seeing yourself behaving more confidently in tense situations will help you realize that you can act confidently and come through those situations with flying colors.

Affirmations

Compose a statement that is totally supportive of your new, natural way of living as a non-smoker. Some suggestions would be statements like the following:

- "Smoking is unhealthy for my body. I make myself healthier every day I don't smoke."
- "I am in charge. I am acting healthier every day."
- "I need my body to live. I give it the respect it deserves."
- "I am naturally a non-smoker."

Your statement should excite you and give you the support you need to make this healthy change.

Find a comfortable place, and sit or lie down. Close your eyes, and spend some time quieting down or doing a relaxation exercise. When you feel calm, slowly repeat your statement to yourself, in silence. Leave five to ten seconds of silence between repetitions. Continue this pattern for five to twenty minutes, until you feel at home with the statement, until you feel as though it is now part of you. Open your eyes, and continue on with your day.

If you choose, you can combine this technique with the visualization technique. Picture yourself in places where you have smoked in the past. This time, however, picture yourself not smoking and acting confidently. As you do this visualization, slowly repeat the affirmation to yourself. Continue for up to twenty minutes, until you feel as though your affirmation is now part of you; then stop.

Positive Statements at Emotionally Charged Times

In the vast majority of cases, smokers reach for a cigarette when they are caught up in emotions like anger or sadness. In fact, the slightest hint of the imminence of an emotionally charged situation will cause smokers to light up because they do not want to allow the emotions to come to the surface.

The moment you feel anger, sadness, uncertainty, depression, or boredom, you need to give yourself encouragement about whatever it is you are doing. Tell yourself that you are doing just fine. If you are becoming anxious about a phone call you must make, tell yourself that the call will go well. If you are bored, reassure yourself that you will come up with an exciting way to spend your time, which will put an end to any feelings of boredom. Do not focus on your emotions or your craving for a cigarette. Instead, focus on your encouraging statement.

Shelly works at an advertising agency, where he is under constant pressure to come up with new ideas for customers' products. He will be working at his desk when the pressure to perform overwhelms him, and he feels the need to take a break. He does this by smoking a cigarette. The feelings of tension indicate that he has some doubts about his ability to perform and cause him to have an even more difficult time being creative.

This in turn leads to more tension. Shelly is clearly caught up in a vicious cycle.

Instead of allowing the tension to mount, Shelly needs to compose a positive statement like "I have fantastic ideas" and repeat it several times; or he could use an effective advertising idea he has devised for another client as a background scene as he makes his statement. By repeating his statement, he will find that his tension decreases, that he is more focused on his assignment, and that he becomes more creative.

These techniques can be a powerful aid to you in your efforts to stop smoking. You need to remember that you are naturally a non-smoker. Smoking is only a way you have found for coping with life's difficult moments. Realize this, and find healthy ways to live every moment of your life. Do not become discouraged if you slip back into your old habit for a day. Simply put out the cigarette, throw the pack away, and recommit yourself to your goal. So many people use one slip as an excuse for starting up again. Don't fall into that way of thinking. Hold on to your knowledge that not smoking will increase your physical health and will offer you the opportunity for greater pleasure and fulfillment in your life.

CHAPTER IX

ELIMINATING

OTHER BAD HABITS

As we discussed in the last chapter, a habit is some behavior that, through constant repetition, no longer requires conscious thought. The mechanics of the behavior have been performed so often that the behavior has entered our unconscious, where it has formed an imprint. We usually do not discover the roots of the habits we develop; and many times the reasons that prompt the behavior now have no connection to the original motivation.

A CHANGE OF DIRECTION

A bad habit is an undesirable, reflexive behavior. As with overeating or smoking, certain people, situations, and emotions trigger the behavior. If the trigger is an emotion, our unconscious reacts so quickly that we do not allow ourselves even to feel the emotion. At the same time, the focus of our attention shifts. No longer are we fully engaged in the activity at hand, since a portion of our attention is being absorbed by the bad habit.

Let me give you an example. Let us assume that you and I are engaged in conversation. You may be giving me 95 percent of your attention. Suddenly, something that is said stirs your unconscious. You raise your hand to your mouth and begin biting your nails. As you do so, the attention you have been giving me plummets to about 40 percent. I have lost you, and our conversation cannot be the same until you have finished biting your nails or until we change the topic that triggered your nail biting in the first place. Once either of these events occurs, your attention will return to its previous level.

At the moment our attention is diverted by the bad habit, we are like a turtle withdrawing into its shell. A turtle responds in this way when it feels threatened. Ordinarily, we are not aware of feeling threatened because the motivating force behind the bad habit is often an unconscious—and erroneous—belief we have about our ability to deal with the person, situation, or emotion that is triggering the fear and consequent bad habit. On an even deeper level is the question of our adequacy. Often in these circumstances we feel that we are not intelligent enough for the conversation, that we are not as attractive as others, that we are not important enough to significantly impact others. Look at the chain of events depicted below:

You're not good enough. (Unconsciously, and maybe consciously, you are carrying this around.)

↓

You encounter a person, emotion, or situation
that triggers your "not good enough" feelings.

You begin doing your bad habit, which allows
part of you to dissociate from the person,
emotion, or situation. This reduces your tension.

Feeling less tension enables you to cope with the
person, emotion, or situation that triggered the
bad feelings.

Let us look at several examples of this. Peter has gotten into the habit of believing he needs two or three drinks in the evening before he can go out socially. On those occasions when he has not imbibed his quota of drinks before going out, he feels tense and self-conscious, and he does not socialize well. *Possible underlying reason:* Feelings of inadequacy. He uses alcohol to help him relax and focus on his good points rather than on his bad ones.

Pauline has the bad habit of talking negatively about other people. In fact, stories about other people seem to take up most of her time and interest. *Possible underlying reason:* Feelings of inadequacy. By criticizing others, Pauline believes she is diverting attention away from herself, from her own inadequacies. She does not think she has anything in her own life in which anyone would be interested.

Jeff is a procrastinator. He promises many things to many people but always seems to be late carrying through on them. *Possible underlying reason:* Feelings of inadequacy. Jeff fears that unless he does things for other people, he will not be liked. At the same time, he doubts his ability to follow through on his promises and fears that these people will criticize, mock, or reject the fruits of his labors.

We are not born with these feelings of inadequacy. Rather, they resulted from oppressive messages we received—and probably continue to receive—from people in our lives. These messages made their way into our unconscious, where they took root and blossomed. At this point, we began to develop bad habits. But to reiterate, bad habits are nothing other than unnatural ways of dealing with situations in which we do not see ourselves as we actually are.

What we need to do is change the erroneous, unconscious messages we have about ourselves in order to eliminate the bad habits we have developed. My three techniques can help get us started.

Visualizations

Just as before, find a comfortable position, close your eyes, and do a relaxation exercise. Think for a minute about where and when you find yourself falling into your bad habit. Now take some time to visualize yourself in one of those places. What you will visualize will have two components: First, you are not doing your bad habit; and second, you are behaving in a totally confident way. Think of someone you perceive as really gutsy, and imagine yourself acting as he/she would act. How would you really like to act in this situation? See yourself that way.

Let me give you an example of this. Dennis bites his nails. One situation in which he does this is when he bowls competitively. At these times he stands off to the side, nervously biting his nails down to the quick. Dennis's underlying fear is that he will not bowl well enough to win the competition.

Dennis can use the technique of visualization to picture himself at the bowling alley, having a good time, and feeling relaxed and confident. He can also visualize himself bowling a fantastic game, again feeling relaxed and confident. He might even imagine himself as Earl Anthony or some other professional bowler.

Affirmations

First, come up with a totally positive statement about yourself, such as "I am relaxed and confident," or "I am doing just fine." Another totally positive statement about yourself could focus on that part of your body involved in your bad habit. If you pull your hair, say to yourself, "My hair is my friend. It grows long and healthy." If you bite your nails, say to yourself, "I am relaxed. My nails grow long and healthy." Now settle into a comfortable position, close your eyes, and do a relaxation exercise. After several minutes, slowly repeat your affirmation to yourself for up to five minutes. Do not say it mechanically. Feel positive emotions about the statement as you repeat it. You can also combine this technique with a visualization. As you picture yourself not doing the habit, repeat your affirmation to yourself, once again feeling positive emotions.

Positive Statements at Emotionally Charged Times

As you become increasingly aware of your bad habit, you may find that you are becoming obsessed with it.

If you bite your nails, you will keep looking at them. If you crack your knuckles, you will start examining them and rationalizing the need to crack them. If you habitually criticize others, you will come up with all sorts of excuses why you should be allowed to do so. Every time you find yourself thinking about doing your bad habit, or if you have just caught yourself in the middle of it, pull your attention away from the habit and ask yourself, "What else can I do right now? What can I do that would be good for me?" In the past, you relied on your bad habit when you were forced to deal with this type of person, emotion, or situation. Now you must reassure yourself that there are alternative ways of coping that are healthy and productive, since there is a part of you that believes that there aren't. Allow yourself to be creative in this situation. Do something you have never done before. Ask a question you have always wanted to ask. When you allow yourself to acknowledge that you have options and when you direct your attention toward them, you will experience a dwindling desire to fall into your old habit.

Jessica is employed as a counselor in a group home for emotionally disturbed adolescents. Each day starts off with a half-hour staff meeting, during which time the staff designs programs for each adolescent and reports on the previous day. As Jessica sits in the meeting, she can feel herself becoming tense, and she unconsciously begins biting her nails.

After attending one of my workshops and hearing my ideas, Jessica walked into her morning meeting the next day and asked herself, "How can I make this meeting worthwhile?" At first she sat there rather blank-minded, then her attention was drawn to her nails. She asked herself again, "How can I make this meeting worthwhile?" She started thinking about the adolescents in the program and realized that a certain treatment for several adolescents just was not working. Actually, she had known this for quite a while but had been too intimidated to say anything, holding the ideas of her fellow-workers in higher esteem than her own. This time, however, she voiced her opinion. Several workers looked at her aghast, but the team leader asked her for more information. She could feel her hand move up toward her mouth, but she caught the reflexive motion in time. Instead of biting her nails, she discussed some behaviors she had observed, as well as some new treatment ideas that were different but that she believed might work.

In the past, she would have allowed the more experienced workers to do the planning, perhaps offering some of her thoughts, shyly and not in depth. However, she now introduced what she knew would be a controversial topic and did not allow herself to succumb to feelings of nervousness. Over time, her nervousness diminished, she felt less of a need to escape through nail biting, and she gained more enjoyment and rewards from taking chances and expressing what she had once kept inside her.

The purpose of these three techniques is to instill new ideas in your unconscious about your ability to handle difficult situations. Once you pull yourself out of your old rut and discover productive, interesting, and healthy ways of coping with people, situations, and emotions that in the past triggered your bad habits, you will enjoy greater creativity and spontaneity in all areas of your life. If you find yourself occasionally slipping back into your old habits, do not let it get you down. Just congratulate yourself for doing so only once in a while, and then pick up where you left off.

CHAPTER X

PUBLIC SPEAKING

WITH A FLAIR

While watching television on Sunday mornings, I have occasionally been riveted by the site of an evangelist moving gracefully across the stage, words flowing articulately and unhaltingly, as he addressed his audience of thousands. He appeared so self-confident, he looked so at ease, that I sighed with envy. Wouldn't it be nice to be able to stand before a sea of humanity, relaxed and self-assured, saying exactly what I wanted to say and moving the crowd with my words? But speaking in front of an audience elicits such fear in most of us that we quake in our boots. I know a rather successful businessman who always appears self-confident and in control of every situation. He is the type of person who is always surrounded by people seeking his advice and listening attentively to his answers. Yet I once saw him stand up before his church congregation to announce his parents' sixtieth wedding anniversary and become so nervous that he forgot his mother's name! Apparently, even those of us who appear self-confident in some areas of our lives can be rattled in others.

Every one of us has the natural ability to get up in front of a group—whether the group consists of several children at a cub scout meeting or thousands of people at a political convention—and speak confidently, creatively, and in a relaxed manner. If we all have that ability, then why do we become so fearful when we are asked to say some words? Most often, we respond in this way because of our feelings of inadequacy. Other times, we experience secondary fears: "People will laugh at me," or "What will I say if someone disagrees with me?" or "What if my mind goes blank?"

Most of the time, we are aware of these surface fears. Underlying each one, however, is the fear that we are not "good enough." It does not matter how self-confident we appear or feel in our lives; if we have difficulty addressing a group, we are harboring some unconscious belief that we are inadequate.

Each of us is born with the natural ability to speak in public. However, we gradually lose that ability as we accept what our authority figures—parents, teachers, other adults—tell us: "Children should be seen and not heard," or "Don't ask so many questions," or "Be quiet and behave yourself." As a result, at a very young age, our unconscious begins to fill with negative messages regarding our speaking out in public; and each time we have to speak in front of a group, we are reminded by our feelings that we should be quiet or that we should not speak up.

If we behave in a way that is consistent with the negative messages our unconscious has been given, if we continue to accept and follow those negative precepts, we only reinforce them, and they become even stronger and more firmly entrenched in our minds. We need to shift our focus in a positive direction by believing that we are capable of speaking in public. As we do so, the impact these negative messages once had upon us will diminish.

Let us look now at how my three techniques can help us speak fluently, creatively, and spontaneously before a group.

Visualizations

When you are fearful of speaking in front of a group, you have consciously or unconsciously a negative picture of how your talk will go. I remember reading somewhere that we do not get what we want, we get what we expect. Picturing yourself different will help you start expecting to be different. When you expect to be different, you *will* be different.

Find a comfortable place, take a moment to quiet down, and close your eyes. Picture yourself at a location where you need to give a talk. Look at the room, look at the people. Imagine that there are many people out there smiling at you, nodding their heads in agreement, and looking very interested in what you are saying. If you have trouble picturing people in the audience, then just know that they are there and that they are interested. Sense support and a positive feeling coming from them. Imagine yourself giving the talk, feeling self-confident and relaxed. You can actually say your speech to yourself at this time or imagine that you are saying it. When you have come to the end of your speech, imagine that you have just delivered the most eloquent and moving speech ever given. People loved it. Imagine hearing their long and hearty applause. They come up to you, shake your hand, and tell you what a wonderful job you have done. Then open your eyes, and relax for a few minutes.

All of these elements are essential to your starting to feel confident and relaxed about public speaking. The elements of this visualization are totally positive, and they contradict the negative pictures lodged in your unconscious. Numerous clients have come to me after having given their talk and excitedly told me that everything they visualized came true. Their words flowed easily, they felt relaxed and self-confident, and afterward they were congratulated and complimented. Their talk had been a success, nothing like the disaster they had anticipated.

Barb is a supervisor of a foster home program within a welfare department in a large metropolitan area. Part of her job is to address large groups on the subject of foster home care and the need for more public participation. She came to me because she was going to be giving a lecture at a national conference on innovative ideas in foster care. She had been nervous during her other talks and was terrified about this one.

I discussed with her the ideas presented in this book, taught her self-hypnosis and the process of visualizations. I then taught her how to visualize herself giving an effective and moving speech, with people applauding her at its conclusion. I worked with her several times to ensure that the visualizations she was doing were totally positive. Her assignment was to do the relaxation technique and visualization the night before her speech. I talked with her when she returned from her trip, and she informed me that she had performed beautifully. She was relaxed, she got her ideas across easily, and the audience was receptive and complimentary.

Affirmations

Choose a totally positive statement that describes how you will feel when you are giving a marvelous talk. Examples would be "I am relaxed and self-confident," or "I have such great ideas to share with these people," or "People enjoy hearing what I have to say."

Find a comfortable place, take a moment to relax, and close your eyes. Do one of the relaxation exercises I have outlined for you or do one of your own. Now spend from one to five minutes repeating your affirmation to yourself. Say it slowly, with feeling, and in silence.

Don owns a photography studio. At a national convention he was scheduled to deliver a speech on new processing techniques. This was the first time he was to address a group, and he was nervous. Don chose the statement "People love what I have to say" as his affirmation. I hypnotized Don; and in the trance, he repeated his affirmation slowly and with warm feelings. He told me that as he repeated his affirmation, he began to feel as if he were in front of a small group of family members, discussing his business. When he actually began his speech at the convention, he was overcome by the same relaxed feeling, and his speech came across in a relaxed, professional manner.

If you wish, you can combine this technique of affirmations with the visualization technique. Picture yourself in front of a group of people and repeat your affirmation a number of times to yourself.

In these situations, the statement and picture enter your unconscious. There, they begin to replace negative messages with memories and expectations of success. I also recommend that you make the same affirmation when you are actually before the group you are about to address. This point leads to our next technique.

Positive Statements at Emotionally Charged Times

As in the last technique, compose a totally positive statement that describes the public speaker you would like to be. Each time you think about giving your talk and feelings of fear begin to wash over you, you are doubting your abilities, usually on an unconscious level. Although those slumbering negative messages have been awakened, you can quiet them with words that are exactly the opposite.

As an added source of income, Nicole began selling a line of kitchen products. Her job required that she make product presentations before groups of people in their homes. As she composed her first presentation, Nicole felt she would have no problem with public speaking. However, upon her arrival at the home, she was stricken with panic. She somehow made it through her talk but was nervous the entire time. She knew she could have done better.

Nicole learned my techniques and chose the statement "I am at home with my presentations." Any time she was in the process of any phase of her work and felt negative emotions, she would immediately turn her attention from them to her affirmation. After repeating her statement a number of times at several presentations, Nicole was convinced that it had added energy to the presentations. With this came added self-confidence and relaxation.

Whether you have just accepted an invitation to speak, planned the talk, or are about to deliver it, any time you start to feel tense and fearful, repeat your affirmation several times. Once you begin to feel relaxed, continue with whatever you were doing. This is a simple technique on the surface, but it is surprisingly powerful in the battle against fear.

I have never had a client who did not experience positive results from these three techniques to eliminate their fear of public speaking. Those same results can be yours. Speaking confidently to people is really quite easy because you will be doing something that comes naturally.

CHAPTER XI

SPORTS

PERFORMANCE

One of the most difficult challenges most athletes face is that of realizing their potential on a consistent basis. It is not surprising that they can demonstrate bursts of athletic brilliance. In 1971 during the Viking–Lions game, when Alan Page of the Minnesota Vikings had a penalty called against him in a key play, Page exploded in anger. On the next three plays, he broke through the defensive line and sacked the quarterback. His playing brilliance continued throughout the rest of the season, and that year he was named Most Valuable Player. Reggie Jackson has earned the nickname "Mr. October" because during the World Series, which is held in October, his performance level seemed to soar.

If these athletes are capable of raising the level of their performance under certain circumstances, are they capable of achieving and maintaining that level, or are they merely fortunate to have been so inspired that their playing exceeded their potential?

MAKING YOUR PERFORMANCE NATURAL

Let us examine the process of learning to play a sport. Through observation and instruction, we gain some knowledge of the mechanics of the sport we are interested in performing. We learn how to hold the ball, how to make different shots, how to mount the horse, how to maintain our balance on the balance beam. Then comes practice. We take what we have been taught and what we have observed, and we consciously translate that knowledge into action. With the repeated physical acting out of the movements involved, a memory of how to perform them makes its way from our conscious to our unconscious; in other words, we develop a habit. If a bowler is asked which is his lead foot, he most likely would have to think about it for a moment before answering. That is because the specific body movement is no longer a conscious one. The athlete no longer needs to carefully proceed with each movement. He does it automatically.

Every athlete who performs at a high level of proficiency is tapping into the knowledge his/her unconscious has stored. No athlete can perform beyond his/her potential because that potential is determined by physical conditioning and that unconscious knowledge.

DEVIATING FROM YOUR POTENTIAL PERFORMANCE

Then why is it that we as athletes so often vacillate in the quality of our performance? Why do some athletes never reach their potential? We have all heard of athletes who coaches thought had great promise, only to be released a year or two later because they never fulfilled those promises. There are several contributing factors, all deriving from our failure to access the knowledge and memories of the excellence of our athletic performance that have entered our unconscious. What we consciously say about ourselves as we prepare for the game or competition significantly affects the outcome. If we question our abilities on a particular day—"I'm going to play poorly today," or "It's too hot to play," or "I know my performance won't be a personal best"— we seriously undermine our confidence in ourselves and increase the likelihood that our predictions will become realities. Such statements also indicate our inability to picture an improvement in the situation.

What happens next is that we swing at the ball, but just a little late; we place our shot carefully, but it falls a little short; we run so quickly we cramp up and have to slow our pace considerably. The negative statements we made previously have caused the pure act of the sport to emerge tainted from our unconscious. We are still going through the motions, but we certainly are not performing up to our potential.

Another reason we perform inconsistently also ties in to our making negative statements. The repetition of negative statements about our ability to perform well creates a buildup of unconscious statements and/or pictures that depict us having performed poorly. In this way, we develop the habit of poor performance. Let me give you an example. Eduardo is a middle-distance runner who lives in Minneapolis. In 1984 he was running a 10K race. In the early part of the race he was running in fifth place. The four men in front of him had always beaten him but he had always beaten the men who were in the pack right behind him, so he decided that he would be happy finishing in fifth place. In a number of earlier races in which he ran against these same runners, he had thought this way, and this self-perception had developed in his unconscious.

NON-POSITIVE INPUT EQUALS NON-POSITIVE OUTPUT

As I have said, negative ideas enter our unconscious through both pictures and words. The pictures come from daydreams about or the actual performance of the sport. The words come from ourselves and/or from others. To combat the negative effects of words, we need to pay attention to what others say about our and/ or our team's performance. Are our teammates being negative? Do they express doubt about performing well, or winning, even before they start? Do those who are benched complain about not playing? This, too, can negatively affect a team's performance. Many marathon runners have told me that as they have stood at the starting line, waiting for the race to begin, they have often heard an onslaught of negative statements—"It's too humid to run," or "I'm too far back in this pack," or "There better be enough water stations." This negativity was contagious. Expressions of doubt, if left unchecked, will enter our unconscious and will fester there until later on when they begin to negatively affect our performance.

The purpose of my techniques is to help you tap into that pure knowledge of how to perform the movements of your sport correctly, to help this behavior become automatic. Let us look at how we can accomplish this.

Visualizations

In the 1984 Winter Olympics, the Mahre brothers, who are giant slalom skiers, as well as several of the luge racers, used the visualization technique I suggest. Every time before Steve or Phil made his downhill run, he would stand poised at the top of the mountain, eyes closed, and visualize himself traversing the course. Scott Hamilton, the U.S. gold medal figure skater, also discussed this same technique. Visualizations can effect positive results, as these athletes can attest.

You can perform this technique individually or in a group setting. Get into a comfortable position, close your eyes, and do a relaxation exercise. Once your body and mind are relaxed, imagine yourself playing your sport perfectly. Make this a high-quality visualization. If your sport is running, see and feel your body running at a smooth, steady pace. See and feel your feet gliding across the surface. When you imagine yourself crossing the finish line, see your time as your personal best. Have people there enthusiastically congratulating you. At several points during this visualization, check how you are feeling. If you are experiencing tension, do another relaxation exercise or take several deep breaths, sighing as you release the air. If you have any doubts, give yourself a totally positive pep talk, then go back and finish the race.

With a number of sports, you can visualize yourself as an animal or bird known for the quality you want to possess. Mark Breland, a 1984 U.S. Olympic gold medal winner in boxing, takes time before a fight to imagine himself standing in the middle of the ring, slowly changing features as he becomes an animal. He sees himself as a lion or tiger stalking his opponent, then moving in.

A runner may see himself/herself as a hawk gliding effortlessly through the air. A long jumper may see himself/herself as a panther or other animal known for its powerful leaps.

If your sport is baseball, tennis, or basketball, visualize yourself playing the game brilliantly. If you are a baseball player, see yourself at home plate in total control of the bat. Hit the ball exactly where you want it to go and run the bases. When you reach home plate, feel good about your accomplishment and congratulate yourself. Remember that the purpose of this visualization is to put the memory of success into your unconscious so that when you are actually performing, you can perform as your memory remembers. The better you perform in your visualization, the better the outcome can be in reality.

If your sport is basketball, imagine yourself playing both offense and defense extraordinarily well. See yourself standing at the free throw line, feeling confident and shooting free throws. Shoot until it feels natural and automatic. Do the same visualization for any shot, from any position.

Now use this same technique for defense. Picture yourself defending against an outstanding offensive player. Imagine that you have an uncanny sense of how to guard this player. Play this game in your mind over and over until you feel comfortable and confident.

"Mac," a sophomore and third-string center on his college basketball team, showed a lot of promise but was not aggressive enough on defense. Wanting to improve his game, he came to me for help. For one-half hour before each game, Mac and I would work on the visualization technique together. In his visualization, Mac would imagine himself playing defense against various exceptional players. He would see himself responding quickly, almost as though he knew what they were going to do before they did it; intercepting passes; batting the ball away; and getting rebounds. With each subsequent game, Mac found that he was becoming increasingly aggressive. In a letter to me at the end of the season, his coach wrote, "Mac came on from third-team center to a starting position. His self-confidence grew tremendously, and I expect great things from him over the next two years."

When you feel good about your visualization, open your eyes and go about your day. Don't think about what you have accomplished because you don't want to distort the purity of it. As I said, the quality of the visualization will determine the quality of the performance. Every great action begins with a great thought. See yourself going through the movements of the game until you feel confident and relaxed, and the movements have become automatic.

Affirmations

Find a comfortable place, close your eyes, and do a relaxation exercise. Before you do, however, come up with a totally positive statement about your performance, such as "I shoot the ball perfectly every time," or "My stroke is smooth and confident," or "I feel relaxed and am playing beautifully." After your body and mind are relaxed, repeat your statement slowly and with feeling for up to twenty minutes. When you feel that your statement has become a part of you, stop and open your eyes.

Jerry is a golfer who has experienced highs and lows in his game. During those holes when he is golfing erratically he becomes very angry, at times throwing his clubs, sometimes farther than his ball has gone. One of his problems is that even as he is setting up for his swing, he is anticipating an errant shot.

Jerry heard about me and decided it could not hurt to try my techniques. After learning self-hynosis, Jerry decided on the affirmation "I am a relaxed, fantastic golfer." At home, the night before he was to go golfing, he would spend twenty minutes doing his induction technique and then repeating his affirmation slowly and with confidence. He later told me that he imagined making the statement twice: first, before a shot; and second, right after the shot. When he was out on the golf course, he found that the moment his affirmation came into his mind, he would immediately relax. There were times, especially at first, when he was about to explode with anger at his performance, but instead he would refocus his attention on the affirmation and give himself encouragement that his swing would be better— and indeed it would be. Jerry found that he no longer anticipated swinging poorly, that his drives were becoming longer and more consistently down the center of the fairway, and that he was beginning to make longer putts as well.

You can combine your statement with the visualization technique. While you are feeling relaxed and picturing yourself performing like a superstar, say your statement occasionally in a relaxed way.

Positive Statements at Emotionally Charged Times

This is an important technique even though you are not in the classical trance state. Pro golfer Dave Stockton was once asked at the beginning of a Masters Tournament which of his opponents he feared the most. His answer to the press was himself. At various times during your sporting event, you may experience certain negative feelings and consequently make negative comments about your performance. If the feelings and/or statements are negative, chances are that your performance will not improve. We have developed the habit of being negative and coming up with excuses why we are not going to do well. This negativity enters our unconscious and prevents us from performing up to our potential. We need to start being aware of how we become negative about our sports performance. Then, when it happens, we can immediately correct our attitude with a positive statement.

New Zealander Lorraine Moller, who runs track and marathons, won the Boston Marathon in 1984. She was using this race as a preliminary to the 1984 Olympics, where she was running in the first Olympic women's marathon. (In the Olympics, she ran a strong race and placed fifth.) I had worked with Lorraine on her running in the past; and when I called to congratulate her on her Boston win, she told me that running the race was the easy part. By that time, she already knew she would win. The difficult part was not allowing herself to have any negative thoughts about her performance. Whenever she thought about the race, she told herself that she was going to run well. If fear or any other negative emotion reared its ugly head, she immediately reassured herself that she was going to run a strong race and win. As a result of this program, she did not permit a negative thought to become established in her mind. Instead, she strengthened the positive. As she said, when the gun went off, she knew she would win. During the race Allison Roe, another New Zealander who has won the Boston and New York City marathons, passed Lorraine and built up quite a lead; however, Lorraine simply reassured herself that she was going to run consistently well and win. Just as she had told herself, later in the race she passed Allison and was never threatened again.

As you reflect on when and how you normally become negative, have on hand some totally supportive statements that you can repeat to yourself. These statements should contradict your negativity. When you are doubting your ability, repeat these statements to yourself, aloud or in silence, whichever feels the most reassuring to you. Then let the feeling go and get on with whatever has to be done.

Another key aspect to which you need pay attention is your posture. As you begin to feel negative, your posture usually will sag. At these moments, stand up straight, and bring your body back to life.

It is best if you practice these techniques a number of times before the day of the sporting event so that you will feel at home with them. When athletes have practiced these three techniques, they have experienced incredible changes in their performance. As they begin to feel more relaxed and self-confident, they start making fewer errors, their hitting or shooting percentage improves, their drives become longer. Whatever the sport, these techniques can work for you. Decide how you wish to implement them in your life and do it. With practice and repetition, you will see that the results are worth the effort.

CHAPTER XII

ILLNESS

AND HEALTH

People seem to have much difficulty accepting or even listening to what I have to say about illness and health, as it goes against everything they have been taught to believe about medicine, disease, and their bodies. The truth is that we are naturally healthy. If we experience an illness or injury, we do so either because of the power of suggestion or because we are mishandling some issue in our lives. What I ask of you is that you follow some of the techniques I suggest for several months, and I promise that you will find your body growing healthier.

A NEW LOOK AT ILLNESS

Many doctors are beginning to change their understanding of the genesis of disease. The doctors postulate that it is probable that throughout our lives, our bodies are attacked by various diseases but we are able to ward off their development because of the health of our bodies' immune systems. This raises a plethora of intriguing questions: Why is it that some of us develop cancer and others do not? Why does one sibling contract the flu every year while the other does not? Extending this to bodily injuries, why are some people accident-prone?

First I want to explore the issue of the power of suggestion. Do you remember being told as a child that you would catch a cold if you went outside not dressed warmly enough? Or that if you visited your friends while they had the flu, you would catch it? Or, if you climbed up into that tree, you would fall and break your arm? Do any of these sound familiar? All of us have heard these dire predictions since we were toddlers.

These suggestions were normally given to us by people who meant a lot to us—our parents or older siblings— and whose advice we normally followed. Because we consciously knew no better, those ideas gradually entered our unconscious, where they began to build a complex of thoughts and beliefs regarding our powerlessness in relation to illness and injury. Many of us will spend our lives working and playing, striving and growing, only to succumb to some germ that attacks our bodies.

Probably a suggestion about illness will have the greatest impact on us if it comes from our doctor or another member of the medical profession. So many people have been told by their doctors that they will have to live with their physical ailment for the rest of their lives, and sure enough most of them do. With that prognosis, they usually stop trying to find a cure and instead resort to prescription drugs, hoping at least to ease their pain.

On the other hand, when doctors assure their patients that they will be themselves in a couple of days, they usually are. If instead of predicting recovery in a couple of days these doctors estimated a week to ten days, a high percentage of their patients would take that long to recover.

These doctors are well intentioned and believe what they say to their patients. However, it is important to bear in mind that a medical prognosis is predicated upon the knowledge or methodology being used to treat that illness. We can accept the way the illness is being treated, and thereby accept the prognosis, or we can seek out those persons whose methodologies offer us different options.

Examining the attitudes toward illness held by those closest to us will give us some insights into our own attitudes toward illness and health. Consider the following:

- How often do you hear the statement "Oh, he is such a sickly person"?
- Are there, or have there been, people in your life who believe that a particular behavior, activity, etc., will result in a particular illness?
- What do you feel when you hear that the flu season is rapidly approaching and you are advised to get a flu shot?
- How do you feel when you are reminded that there is a history of a certain disease in your family?
- What do you say to yourself about an illness when you start feeling poorly?

- Are you described by others or yourself as being clumsy?

Our answers to these questions will clue us in to the extent to which our own attitudes toward illness have been—and continue to be—molded by suggestions.

PERSONAL POWER VS. THE POWER OF SUGGESTION

Now let us look at how you can combat suggestions about illness. First, you must wholeheartedly reject any prediction or warning that you are going to get sick "if. . . ." It is best if you learn to be aware of and reject these statements within thirty seconds of receiving them. An effective approach is the following:

Jerry: Everyone has the flu. I wonder when we'll get it.

Kathy: I'm not going to get it. I'm healthy, and I intend to stay that way.

Make your response pleasant but firm. Live by your own rules, and let others live by theirs. If you choose, you do not have to say anything at all. You will find that these suggestions will come from all sources—from parents and friends and even the media. Whatever the source, reject the suggestion and reassure yourself that you are healthy.

MISHANDLING DAILY ISSUES

We also fall ill because we are mishandling some important issues in our lives. Let us look for a moment at

Ross, who is an inveterate worrier. He worries about his job, regardless of whether or not it is going well. He worries about finances, his kids, his wife's fidelity. He has trouble verbalizing his concerns, so instead he swallows them, and they sit in the pit of his stomach, eating away at its lining. It is no wonder that Ross has developed a painful ulcer.

What is natural and healthiest for us is to face problems as they present themselves, effect some sort of healthy resolution, and then move on. When we do not proceed in this way, we suffer, for if problems are not resolved on a psychological level, they will demand to be worked out on a physical one.

Let us look at Dale, a professional writer in his mid-thirties, who recently fell ill. Dale had a terrible headache; his eyes and joints ached so much they virtually cried out in pain; and he had chills running through his body, which felt as if it had been poisoned. Thinking about the significance of these symptoms, Dale realized that for two days prior to their onset, he had been having a lot of trouble with some men he had hired to work on his house. They had failed to show up as scheduled and to call when they were supposed to; when they finally did show up, their equipment, which was in poor condition, kept breaking down. Every time Dale thought about these workers, which was frequently during those days, he found himself growing angrier and angrier, complaining that he did not deserve this treatment. Dale suddenly became aware that this negativity, which he was not expressing or resolving, was seething within him and poisoning his body. Once he began to deal with

PICTURE ME PERFECT

his feelings about his predicament, his body began to feel better.

Let us look at another situation. Jeannie feels the need to rescue others and solve their problems, and she seems to attract people whose lives are fraught with issues that need to be resolved. Yet, at the same time, she criticizes everyone who seeks her help and complains that she never has any time for herself. After a number of years of rescuing people, she began to develop problems with her shoulders and upper back. There are clichés in our culture about "carrying everyone's problems on our shoulders" and "shouldering someone else's responsibilities." Clearly, that is what Jeannie has been doing; but coexisting with this need to heal has been her anger and resentment at the amount of time and energy it has demanded of her. Because she was unable to deal with this conflict, it went unattended and an imbalance was created within her that began to manifest itself on a physical level.

As is evident in Jeannie's case, very often the area of our bodies that is ill or injured is symbolic and can tell us something about the issues in our lives that need attention. My wife, Marilyn, and I have written a book, *Illness, Thoughts, and Change*, in which we list a number of illnesses and possible unresolved issues that are causing the illness. Below are a number of them.

ILLNESS	POSSIBLE ISSUES
Acne	Needing to break out of an intolerable situation; feeling frustrated. Being angry at feeling trapped and fearing

what lies ahead should you become free.

Allergies	Wishing to escape but feeling uncomfortable about doing so. Feeling powerless. Feeling afraid to adapt or to make changes.
Appendicitis	Experiencing difficulty making a transition. Holding on to a lot of past negativity.
Asthma	Housing buried struggles that exist from being smothered by significant others in your life. Wishing to break loose.
Bladder Problems	Being unable to release your emotions. (For instance, you swallow your anger like a bitter pill and never deal with it. It stays inside you, maybe coming out in the form of burning urine.)
Blood Poisoning	Feeling that nothing is going right for you. Being unable to make some positive changes. Being involved in an unhealthy, nonsupportive primary or secondary relationship.
Broken Bones (General)	Internalizing shattering experiences in your life. Being discouraged from experiencing or continuing to pursue certain activities.

(Legs/Feet)	Lacking support in your life. (Everything you stand for is being questioned or shattered: "I no longer have a leg to stand on.")
(Hands)	Experiencing major disappointment or hurt in something or someone you hold dear.
(Arms)	Losing your hold on things or people you once held close. Being afraid of or disappointed in things for which you have been striving.
Bursitis	Being afraid to edge your way into something in your life. (Maybe you were bruised during this process and are now backing off.)
Charley Horses	Being tied up in knots about something. Being unable to make a decision. Being conflicted about achieving.
Cold Sores	Not being honest about your feelings. Wanting to express your feelings but not feeling free to do so.
Constipation	Experiencing a tightness, a lack of movement, in your life. Lacking generosity. Being unable to give. Fearing the future.
Diabetes	Not having enough sweetness or joy in your life, or not feeling comfortable about having it.

Diarrhea	Being unwilling to hold on to anything in your life. Not maximizing potential value by letting go too soon.
Eczema	Believing that your value is skin-deep. Wanting to participate but not putting much into it. Looking on from the outside; afraid to join in.
Epilepsy	Fearing life's path. Needing to learn how to persevere and face your issues.
Flu	Needing to retire, to escape, from your life. Being poisoned by unhealthy thoughts and/or actions.
Hayfever	Not wanting to participate in certain activities but feeling coerced into doing so. Being irritated about this but holding the irritation in.
Heart Problems	Holding on to emotional pains and disappointments. Dealing ineffectively with disappointments.
High Blood Pressure	Deeply questioning your ability to deal with life's issues. Fearing that your success will not last.
Hyperventilation	Tapping into old and painful issues. Needing to retain control.
Impotence	Fearing intercourse and/or its results (closeness, pregnancy, self-disclosure). Feeling inadequate or doubting your ability to please your partner.

123

Insomnia	Doubting your abilities regarding what you accomplished during the day. Worrying about what needs to be faced the following day.
Menstrual Disorders	Not feeling good about being a woman. Having unhealthy ideas about your body. Being disappointed in sex and/or romance.
Muscular Dystrophy	Acutely fearing some action you desire to undertake. Wishing to escape, to surrender.
Neck Problems	Being inflexible, rigid. Being unwilling to look at others' viewpoints.
Paralysis	Being terrorized by fear and unwilling to admit it. Feeling tired of responsibilities but unsure how to become free of them.
Pneumonia	Feeling powerless. Wishing to surrender.
Psoriasis	Becoming hardened to certain areas of your life. Fearing involvement; wishing to remain separate.
Stomachaches	Being inflexible, unwilling to digest new ideas. Being exposed to unhealthy belief systems (racism, sexism).
Teeth	"Biting off more than you can chew." Feeling angry about your inability to take more into your life.
Throat (sore)	Being judgmental, self-righteous, or critical of others. Listening to others

	judge and not speaking out when you disagree.
Varicose Veins	Experiencing rocky times. Getting bogged down on some issues.
Warts	Feeling unattractive. Having a major area in your life (family, work, friends) that is unhealthy/non-supportive.

If your illness is listed, check the possible causes that appear next to it. Think about them awhile; if one feels right, then start working on that issue. Look for new and different ways to deal with it.

If the illness in which you are interested is not listed, I have a technique of self-exploration that will help you gain insight into it. Find a comfortable place, close your eyes, and do a relaxation exercise. What I want you to do next relies upon the fact that a part of your consciousness knows the reason behind your illness. Therefore, to tap into this, move your focus down to where your illness is located and ask it in silence, "What do I need to handle differently in my life for you to go away?" Ask yourself this once or twice, and then just wait. The quieter your mind is, the clearer the answer that emerges will be. Do not be impatient or judgmental. Take whatever answer you receive from your unconscious as a gift and act on it. Learn to deal with your issues in healthier and more creative ways.

Another visualization you can do will provide you with some relief and will shorten the life of the illness, but it will not address the cause. Therefore, you should use this technique for some relief from the illness or together with the visualization just discussed.

There is a healing component to breathing and focusing the body's natural energy. Find a comfortable place, close your eyes, and do a relaxation exercise. When you feel your body and mind have become quieted, then focus on your breathing. As you breathe through your nose, focus on the air. Feel it travel all the way from your nose to your lungs. Know that this is a healing energy. Now, direct this air in through your nose and down to the area of your body where the illness or injury is located. Let the air surround and fill this area. Feel the air taking the cells apart and putting them back together again, this time in a healthy way. Continue for three to four minutes, and then open your eyes. Do not question whether or not this process is working. Just trust in it, and you will see the results.

Wouldn't it be wonderful if you did not succumb to illness as you have in the past? Follow these techniques, and you won't. I feel the need to say that I am not advocating that you not see your doctor if you become ill. I do myself. But you will discover that there are many illnesses for which you do not seek medical treatment. These illnesses provide excellent opportunities for you to use the techniques I have presented. These techniques can also be applied in conjunction with medical treatment. Your doctor's work is an excellent supplement to your own healing powers. Your body is a beautiful instrument, and it was not meant to get ill provided it is well taken care of by you.

CHAPTER XIII

HANDLING DEATH
IN A HEALTHY WAY

We have so much death to face during our lives, and how we face death affects our ability and willingness to face life. Do we run from death? Do we deny it as a reality for ourselves and those around us? Or do we try to accept it?

Walter's aunt, who was also his godmother, died very unexpectedly one evening of heart failure. At her funeral, Walter found himself surrounded by more than fifty people who, for the most part, were related in some way, and he was overwhelmed by the realization that only one person in that entire group would live to see the others die before him/her. This person would attend the wake and funeral for every family member present. What an overpowering thought that was for him.

In the days that followed his aunt's death, Walter often thought about her. She had been experiencing some family problems at the time of her death and had been calling him for some advice, some of which she took. But then life became more hectic than usual and Walter had not talked with her for a number of weeks. In his quiet moments he would wonder how she was doing. Then he heard of her death, and was filled with sadness, shock, and guilt.

Walter had been to my workshops and had learned self-hypnosis. One evening at home, he closed his eyes, pictured his aunt in front of him, and began talking to her. He told her about his pain and guilt about not helping her as perhaps he should have; and she responded, giving him words of reassurance. They talked back and forth, and what she said brought much peace to Walter's heart.

Whenever someone close to us dies, some of our reactions are similar to those children experience when their parents go through a divorce. Very often their reactions are (1) to blame themselves for the divorce, (2) to withdraw from their parents, as well as from any future stepparents, to avoid pain in case they too should leave, and (3) to idealize their parent, which precludes their establishing a relationship with any future stepparent.

THE ISSUE OF SELF-BLAME

Let us look at an example that demonstrates the first reaction, that of self-blame. Tina's father died from lung cancer at the age of fifty-three. He had been a heavy smoker all of his adult life. Although Tina had asked him a number of times to stop smoking, he always refused, insisting that he enjoyed it too much. Then one day the cancer was detected, and within a year he was dead. Tina experienced a great deal of anger once the cancer was detected. At first, the anger was directed toward her father, then at herself. Why hadn't she demanded that he stop smoking? Why hadn't she walked out of the room every time he smoked in order to force him to quit? Why hadn't she stolen his cigarettes and thrown them away whenever she saw them on the table?

Tina came to see me two years after the death, still feeling angry. Using techniques presented in this book, I quieted her body and her conscious thoughts. After several sessions, she was able to visualize her father after the cancer had been detected. She told him of her anger about his smoking and about what it would mean to lose him. She told him what she had done to try to make him stop smoking and her fantasies about what she should have done. During these sessions she cried endlessly. She visualized him holding her and apologizing for having caused her such pain but there would not have been anything she could have done that would have stopped his smoking. He appreciated her attempts; but if she had been any more forceful, he probably would have become angry and pulled away from her—and continued smoking. He told her that if she ever needed to hear his voice, she should just listen, and he would be there offering her his support.

WITHDRAWING FOR SELF-PROTECTION

The second reaction concerns withdrawing ourselves from others to avoid the pain if they should die. This is a terribly destructive and painful pattern because it is contrary to our natural instincts to interact with people. If we distance ourselves to avoid hurt, we cut ourselves off from one of our basic needs.

Julie's husband, Doug, was killed instantaneously in a car accident when they were both twenty-seven years old. During the four years following his death, she eliminated most close relationships from her life. She no longer communicated with Doug's family, no longer socialized with the friends they both knew. She worked with her sister, with whom she would spend her lunch hour, but she would converse with no one else. Occasionally a man at work showed interest in her, but she would only turn pale and become very quiet. At some point she became very depressed, and her sister, sensing her pain and observing her lifestyle, urged her to see me.

After altering her level of awareness by quieting her mind and body, I had her choose a place where she would feel comfortable and picture herself there with Doug one day before the accident. I then encouraged her to share her feelings with him—to tell him about her love for him, about the things she has enjoyed about the relationship, about the ways in which she has grown since they have been together. We repeated this visualization during a number of sessions. Sometimes she would need coaxing to express these feelings because they opened up deep hurt inside of her. At other times she would feel a burst of anger; and when she was through expressing it to him, she would once again talk about her love and the strengths she had developed during their relationship. Next, I had her visualize the accident again, realizing Doug's life was now gone. However, as she saw the accident I then also had her imagine Doug meeting her right after it had occurred. She was in a sense meeting him at the door as he was on his way out. At this point, I once again encouraged her to say whatever she wanted to him. Tell him about her anger, tell him about her fears about being alone. I then instructed her to sense being hugged by him. Physical touching in this type of scene is very important because it seems to open many floodgates and release any repressed emotions. It also forces the person to feel the closeness, the warmth, and the intimacy of the relationship. Next, I had her tell him what she had enjoyed in the relationship, why she had remained in it, what he had given her and she, him.

The movement of the sessions alternated between the emotions that prevented her from thinking to her thoughts about the relationship. Once these emotions were experienced, it was possible for her to begin thinking clearly again. At last, it was time for Tina to say goodbye to Doug, yet to know that he would be there in thought whenever she needed him. Going through this experience released Tina from the past and allowed her to look toward the future. She will continue to find life difficult and frightening for a while, but this experience will have given her a little push in the right direction.

SELF-PROTECTION THROUGH IDEALIZATION

The third reaction we can have to the death of a loved one is to idealize him/her, to exaggerate beyond all realistic proportion his/her strengths and attributes so that no one else could ever meet those standards. This

attitude prevents us from establishing viable relationships with other people and—presumably—safeguards
us against future loss and pain.

Bill, age forty-seven, came to me five years after his
wife, Naomi, had died, saying he was still depressed
about the loss. He claimed that he wanted to be in a
relationship, but he always found himself comparing his
dates to Naomi, and his dates always came out on the
losing end. Bill told me that Naomi had been a fantastic
schoolteacher, who was loved and respected by students
and colleagues alike. Naomi always knew what Bill was
thinking, even before he said anything. She was an
accomplished cook, a fabulous tennis player, and a true
companion. He could not recall their ever having had
one serious argument in their seventeen years of marriage. He could not praise her enough.

I placed Bill in a tranquil state of body and mind, and
had him imagine Naomi sitting beside him. I told him
to take as much time as he needed to tell her how much
he appreciated her and everything she had done for
him. When he was through, I told him to discuss with
her what he needed to accomplish in his life. What did
she hope for him? How could he continue to grow after
she had left? In the conversation he had with her, she
told him that when he was ready, she wanted him to
enter into another relationship. She told him that there
were women out there who would be good to him and
good for him. This caused Bill to shed some tears, and
in his mind Naomi took him into her arms and encouraged him by this act to let go of his pain.

We shared this experience several times. I would help
Bill into a relaxed state, and then he would speak with

Naomi. At one session after he had cried, I asked him to look her in the eyes and tell her that as she had needed to move on, now so did he. They embraced for a long time, he released her, and she walked away. But she would never be far away in case he needed her.

In subsequent sessions, I had Bill imagine himself with a woman he had dated several times. In the visualization, I had him tell her that he was going to begin seeing some of the wonderful qualities she possessed. Even before Bill came out of the trance, one of her nicest qualities flashed into his mind, something he had been blocking all along.

Now let us look at how we can apply these three techniques. While they need to incorporate certain key elements, you must have the freedom to modify them to meet your own needs. However, be careful not to modify them as a defense.

Visualizations

Find a quiet place, lie or sit down, and close your eyes. Do a relaxation exercise. Now picture yourself someplace where you feel comfortable and safe. See the person who has died sitting right in front of you. Look into his/her eyes for a few seconds. If you have any feelings of guilt about this person's death, express them. Do you feel in any way responsible for his/her death? Do not judge your feelings, just express them. Listen carefully to what he/she has to say. Next express any feelings of anger you may have. Was the person who died in any way responsible for his/her own death? For instance, if the death was caused by a car accident, did this person always drive too fast? Your anger does not have to make any sense, just express it. Also, your anger may not be at all related to the cause of this person's death. Instead, it may have been precipitated by something he/she did or said and you never had the opportunity to express how you felt about it. For instance, Carolyn's father sexually abused her on a number of occasions during her teenage years. He died before she was able to get a grip on what had happened and confront him about it. With the visualization technique, she would need to express her rage and her pain about having been raped before she could express any other feelings.

Next, talk about your sadness. What is it going to be like being alone? When tears come, do not hold them back. You do not have to wipe your eyes or nose. Many times that movement can be an escape and can lessen the intensity of the experience. Talk with the person about your relationship. What did you like about it? What did he/she give to the relationship? If you are angry with the person, you may deny him/her any importance. What did you contribute to the relationship? We also tend to minimize the importance of our own input. You must come up with answers to these last two questions. What aspects of the relationship did you not like?

Next, tell the person what you intend to do with your life. The death of someone close to you can be seen as an end or as a beginning. You are not betraying your loved one by seeing his/her death as a beginning. Death means change because someone who filled some space in your life can no longer do so. The space must be filled with something, even if it is depression. Presumably, you will find a healthier substitute. Ask the person what he/she wishes for you. Give this person a chance to talk, and you will hear what you were unable to hear before.

When you feel a lull in the conversation, give the person a good, long hug and say goodbye. Watch this person then walk away.

You may need to repeat this visualization several times. As I said earlier, give yourself freedom to modify it. You may decide to devote the first visualization entirely to expressing only your anger. If that is what you need, then do it. The purpose of this visualization is to say what you never finished saying or even started to say in the first place. Once you do, you can do something that is natural, and that is to go on living.

Affirmations

This technique and the one that follows should be used only after the visualization technique has been repeated several times and you have worked out most of your emotions about the death but some unresolved feelings and/or issues remain.

First, compose two short sentences. An example would be, "I love John. I now release him and continue to grow." The first sentence needs to state what you are feeling for the person you have lost. It is important to express these feelings rather than risk denying them. The second sentence needs to state that you are releasing the person and the reason why you are doing so. By holding the deceased person to you, you remain in the past and avoid being totally engaged in the present. The second part of this sentence ("and continue to grow") states your intention, your determination, to follow a positive path rather than remain where you are and wonder what direction to take. When you have composed two sentences (or decided to take mine), find a comfortable place, close your eyes, and do a relaxation exercise. Next, bring the deceased person into your awareness for a few seconds. You do not need to visualize the person at all. It is just important that you put the feeling of him/her in your mind. Take your two statements and repeat them slowly for three or four minutes. When you feel that period of time is up, stop, sit for a few seconds, then open your eyes.

The purpose of this technique is not to erase that person from your mind but to prevent you from continuing to fearfully cling to him/her. You will release the chains, not the memories, and move on with your life.

Positive Statement at Emotionally Charged Times

For this technique you may use the same two sentences you used for the second technique or compose two others. You may find that something in your life will trigger you into the memory of the deceased person, and feelings of sadness will re-emerge. These feelings are natural and healthy ones. But when they linger on indefinitely and you have taken a leave of absence from the rest of your life, they become unnatural and unhealthy. Driving by a place the two of you frequented or receiving a gift he/she once surprised you with may trigger these emotions. At these emotionally charged times, you can apply this technique. Again, this technique works best once you have used the first technique on a number of occasions.

When you find yourself suddenly feeling sad about your loss, repeat your two sentences to yourself several times. If the sadness is still there, repeat them again, maybe aloud. If it is anger you are feeling, tell yourself you have every right to be angry, and then release the anger. Focus on the present. Notice the colors, the people, everything around you.

So often when someone close to us dies we think our whole purpose in life dies as well. The higher truth is that it is not so. Death of a loved one is painful, but it is an experience none of us can escape. The use of these three techniques will help you find your way back to the path of life, not by abandoning your loved one, not by forgetting him/her, but by loving and rediscovering the importance of your own life.

EPILOGUE

"Fly high like an eagle, soar like a bird" are words from John Denver's song "Calypso." Each of us deserves to have this as our theme: to soar high above the problems to which we have clung in the past and which have kept us from living creative, loving, and energetic lives.

In Chapter 5, where I focused on relaxation and confidence, I mentioned Phil, who had come to see me because of the turmoil in his marriage and on his job. I described how he had sat in my office, unable to look into my eyes because he felt so terrible about himself. Many years before, Phil was like any other young, healthy child, with great hopes for the future. Each morning he would naturally spring from his bed to share day-long adventures with his playmates. Yet, he had become a man who had lost the spring in his walk, his sense of adventure, his love of people, his smile, his soul. He now listened to the echoes from that crust of negativity that had built up within him over the years. He accepted and believed that he was the person others in his life had defined him to be.

To be happy, we must be positive; and for that positiveness to be long-lasting, it must come across through every aspect of our being: our posture, smile, assertiveness; our acknowledgment that if we can dream, we can realize that dream; and our willingness to use the power of our mind to make the changes we wish to make. Phil made those changes once he became aware of several truths: He was a worthwhile human being; he had fantastic ideas; and he deserved the support of others in his life. Phil began to feel more relaxed with people when he started to interact honestly with them. He realized that many people did give him support; and those who did not, he could set straight with his rediscovered interpersonal skills.

There was not one aspect of Phil's life that did not change. He and his wife went through some turbulent times, but they found a common thread for existence and built happiness from there. Phil began asserting himself at work and eventually left his job to open his own shop. As he learned to set aside his negativity and to use the three techniques I have presented, an air of relaxation surrounded him. From that point on, he had the ability to bring every dream he had into his life.

Look at the people on the street and those in your life. You will see a continuum of health that ranges from the smiling, creative, energetic child to the unhealthy, dirty, "down and out" individual who staggers along the sidewalk with blurred vision. This continuum can also be perceived from a different perspective: simply, a continuum of varying degrees of negativity that have entered the unconscious of all of us. All of us have our places along this continuum; and for all our sakes, I hope we are closer to that fresh, young child. The closer we are to that child, the more support we will give each other. The more we resemble that defeated individual, the more negative and complaining we are about each other.

By using my three techniques, we will get through whatever negativity we encounter and will not allow ourselves to be controlled by it. We will attain heights we never dreamed of attaining; and our sense of freedom and love of life will naturally and positively affect those with whom we come into contact.

Our minds are tools whose powers go virtually untapped. Through the power of words and imagery, we can access that power and apply it creatively in our lives. Some say the power is psychological; others say it is metaphysical. Whatever the source, the results will be the same—positive change within our lives.

I have addressed a variety of issues that touch many areas of life. Use the techniques I have given you to work on any of these issues, as well as any others that exist for you. Make John Denver's words "fly high like an eagle, soar like a bird" become your theme. Fly high in your hopes and expectations. Don't accept such statements as "You have to be realistic," or "You need to slow down." Soar above the limitations and negativity that others accept and pass on. Do not accept what you have become but, instead, strive for what you can be. Limit the suffering imposed by illness in your life and maximize health and well-being. Fill your life with experiences that bring you fulfillment and happiness, experiences you can cherish yourself or share with others. Do not permit yourself to be manipulated by those around you or by the negativity within your unconscious. You have learned how to harness the powers of your unconcsious; now do so. Fly high and soar.